Exploring the Civil-Military Divide over Artificial Intelligence

JAMES RYSEFF, ERIC LANDREE, NOAH JOHNSON,
MADHUMITA GHOSH-DASTIDAR, MAX IZENBERG, SYDNE NEWBERRY,
CHRISTOPHER FERRIS, MELISSA A. BRADLEY

Prepared for the Office of Net Assessment
Approved for public release; distribution unlimited

NATIONAL DEFENSE RESEARCH INSTITUTE

For more information on this publication, visit **www.rand.org/t/RRA1498-1**.

About RAND

The RAND Corporation is a research organization that develops solutions to public policy challenges to help make communities throughout the world safer and more secure, healthier and more prosperous. RAND is nonprofit, nonpartisan, and committed to the public interest. To learn more about RAND, visit www.rand.org.

Research Integrity

Our mission to help improve policy and decisionmaking through research and analysis is enabled through our core values of quality and objectivity and our unwavering commitment to the highest level of integrity and ethical behavior. To help ensure our research and analysis are rigorous, objective, and nonpartisan, we subject our research publications to a robust and exacting quality-assurance process; avoid both the appearance and reality of financial and other conflicts of interest through staff training, project screening, and a policy of mandatory disclosure; and pursue transparency in our research engagements through our commitment to the open publication of our research findings and recommendations, disclosure of the source of funding of published research, and policies to ensure intellectual independence. For more information, visit www.rand.org/about/principles.

RAND's publications do not necessarily reflect the opinions of its research clients and sponsors.

Published by the RAND Corporation, Santa Monica, Calif.
© 2022 RAND Corporation
RAND® is a registered trademark.

Library of Congress Control Number: 2022908108
ISBN: 978-1-9774-0902-7

Cover: Design-Carol Ponce, Ariel Owings/U.S. Air Force, Jamesteohart/Adobe Stock.

Limited Print and Electronic Distribution Rights

About This Report

Artificial intelligence (AI) is anticipated to be a key capability for enabling the U.S. military to maintain its military dominance. The U.S. Department of Defense (DoD)'s engagement with leading high-tech private sector corporations, for whom the military is a relatively small percentage of their customer base, provides a valuable conduit to cutting-edge AI-enabled capabilities and access to leading AI software developers and engineers. This study conducted a survey of software developers at leading technology corporations to learn their views toward the U.S. defense community and their willingness to contribute to AI-related projects for DoD.

The research reported here was completed in October of 2021 and underwent security review with the sponsor and the Defense Office of Prepublication and Security Review before public release.

RAND National Security Research Division

This research was sponsored by the U.S. Department of Defense's Office of Net Assessment and conducted within the Acquisition and Technology Policy Center and the Forces and Resources Policy Center of the RAND National Security Research Division (NSRD), which operates the National Defense Research Institute (NDRI), a federally funded research and development center sponsored by the Office of the Secretary of Defense, the Joint Staff, the Unified Combatant Commands, the Navy, the Marine Corps, the defense agencies, and the defense intelligence enterprise.

For more information on the RAND Acquisition and Technology Policy Center, see www.rand.org/nsrd/atp; and for more information on the RAND Forces and Resources Policy Center, see www.rand.org/nsrd/frp or contact the centers' directors (contact information provided on the web page).

Acknowledgments

We would like to thank Laura Werber, Elizabeth Sayers, Michael Spirtas, Yuna Wong, and Cortney Weinbaum for their assistance in preparing the survey instrument. We would also like to thank Amanda Muller, Gillian Hadfield, and Jovana Jankovic for their assistance in publicizing this study. Lauren Skrabala created graphics and visualizations to greatly improve this report. Finally, we would also like to thank our reviewers (Jack Shanahan, Maria Lytell, Igor Mikolic-Torreira, Molly McIntosh, Joel Predd, Howard Shatz, Chris Mouton, and Brodi Kotila) for all of their helpful insights and questions.

Summary

Background

Many defense experts in the United States believe that implementing artificial intelligence (AI) to its fullest potential could be a decisive element in maintaining the United States' military dominance. However, despite the potential importance of this technology to the U.S. Department of Defense (DoD), military research and development funding for AI represents only a small portion of the total investment in this technology.[1] Instead, most of the recent breakthroughs in creating AI algorithms have come from software companies that focus on the commercial market. And, unlike traditional defense contractors, for whom DoD is a significant if not primary customer, DoD constitutes a relatively small percentage of the overall customer base for most of these high-tech software companies. Because these companies employ some of the leading AI talent and have built some of the most-capable technical frameworks, drawing on these experts' talents could benefit DoD's efforts to leverage AI for its own transformation.

This study aimed to capture and understand the views of software engineers and other technical staff working in the private sector about potential DoD applications using AI.

Approach

To assess the views of software engineers in the private sector about potential DoD applications of AI, a RAND research team conducted a survey that presented a variety of scenarios describing how the U.S. military might employ AI and asked respondents to describe their comfort level with using AI in these ways. The scenarios varied several factors, including their degree of distance from the battlefield, the destructiveness of the action, and the degree of human oversight over the AI algorithm.

Additionally, the survey examined several factors that might have helped influence respondents' views, specifically

- trust in major institutions of society, such as the federal government, the military, and U.S. technology companies.
- perceived level of threat from strategic competitors and other global problems potentially requiring a military response.
- the news sources that individuals in the software engineering community tend to rely on to inform them about global affairs.

---

[1] International Data Corporation (IDC) estimated the global AI market at 327.5 billion dollars in 2021, while DoD spent only 1.4 billion dollars on AI contracts in fiscal year 2020. This understates the total disparity, because the IDC estimate does not include money spent internally by corporations on their own investments in AI or the money corporations have spent on acquiring AI startups (see IDC, "IDC Forecasts Improved Growth for Global AI Market in 2021," Needham, Mass., press release, February 23, 2021; and Justin Doubleday, "New Analysis Finds Pentagon Annual Spending on AI Contracts Has Grown to $1.4B," *Inside Defense*, September 24, 2020).

The survey was fielded from December 2020 to April of 2021[2] and received 1,178 responses, the largest number of participants ever recruited for a study focused on these topics and on this community of experts. These participants came from three distinct survey populations.

- 726 software engineers and other technology workers[3] from three large software corporations—specifically Google, Microsoft, or Amazon—referred to hereafter as *Silicon Valley Employees.*
- 252 alumni of universities with top-ranking computer science (CS) departments who do not work for either the large Silicon Valley software companies or for companies that frequently accept defense contracts; these respondents are hereafter referred to as the *Alumni of Top CS Universities* population.
- 200 software engineers working at traditional defense contractors; these respondents are hereafter referred to as the *Defense Industrial Base* (DIB) population.

Surveying both the Silicon Valley Employees and Alumni of Top CS Universities helped provide insight into whether the former population is representative of the broader software industry or whether they have unique concerns compared with other tech experts. The DIB population served as a useful benchmark for comparing responses from the other two groups.

Key Findings

There does not appear to be an unbridgeable divide between Silicon Valley and DoD: Overall, the results of the survey indicate that there are more similarities than differences in attitudes across all three of the survey populations toward military use of AI. Most survey respondents from all populations reported that they were comfortable with a wide variety of potential military applications for AI.

- A majority of Silicon Valley Employees and Alumni of Top CS Universities respondents were comfortable deploying AI algorithms that would recommend lethal battlefield actions for U.S. service members to act on (i.e., human in the loop).
- Overwhelming majorities of participants from all populations supported applying AI algorithms to protect soldiers on the battlefield from unmanned threats, such as enemy missiles and improvised explosive devices, or to augment military functions supporting the battlefield, such as supply chain management.
- As a group, private sector technology workers who are not employed within the DIB perceive global threats similarly to their counterparts at defense contractors, and they believe that using military force is justified to respond to many kinds of aggressive behavior from U.S. adversaries or to protect U.S. allies.

All in all, these results illustrate that most of the United States' AI experts do not oppose the basic mission of DoD or the use of AI for many military applications.

There is a meaningful difference in the comfort level for AI applications that involve the use of lethal force: At the same time, most respondents—including a majority of software engineers from the DIB—were

---

[2] As with any survey, real-world events that occurred during the sample period have the potential to affect its results. The researchers avoided fielding the survey during the 2020 presidential election in an attempt to avoid affecting the results; however, significant events still occurred during the survey period. The most impactful of these events are noted in the analysis.

[3] The survey focused on software engineers but also included a variety of other roles at the company to determine whether technical staff saw these issues differently from nontechnical staff. Eighty percent of survey respondents in this population were software developers; 10 percent were other technical roles, such as software testers, site reliability engineers, or product managers; and the remaining 10 percent were nontechnical staff.

uncomfortable with allowing AI algorithms to take lethal actions without human oversight, even if it was necessary to save the lives of U.S. military personnel. These data also show a meaningful shift in the comfort level between the Silicon Valley Employees and Alumni of Top CS Universities compared with software engineers from the DIB over AI applications that involve the use of lethal force even when supervised by humans. Although a majority of Silicon Valley Employees and Alumni of Top CS Universities feel comfortable with human-in-the-loop uses of lethal force by AI algorithms, approximately one-third of these groups feel uncomfortable with these potentially lethal uses for AI. Using AI algorithms to identify foreign terrorists splits both the Silicon Valley Employees and Alumni of Top CS Universities respondents nearly evenly between those who are comfortable and uncomfortable using AI for this purpose. In contrast, less than one-fifth of respondents from the DIB feel uncomfortable with man-in-the-loop uses of lethal force and only one-quarter feel uncomfortable with using AI to identify foreign terrorists.

Tech workers have low levels of trust in leaders—even their own: The survey results also provided insights as to what factors might influence opinions on these topics. To begin with, survey respondents from all survey populations reported low levels of trust in leaders of organizations—even chief executive officers of technology companies. This reflects the typical organizational culture of software engineering organizations that often emphasizes individual autonomy and creativity instead of processes and hierarchy. Additionally, Silicon Valley Employees and Alumni of Top CS Universities respondents reported a significantly lower level of trust in the military compared with respondents from the DIB, with approximately 20 percent fewer respondents expressing a high degree of trust in DoD, military officers, and civil servants working for the department.

Tech workers are most concerned about cyber threats: When asked to rate their concerns about various threats to national security, survey respondents expressed the greatest concern about cyberattacks:

- More than 66 percent of participants in each population rated cyberattacks as critical threats to the United States.
- None of the other global threats that might require a military response were perceived to be as urgent a priority, with less than half as many respondents considering these to be critical threats.
- More than 75 percent of respondents from all three populations also regarded China and Russia as serious threats to the United States.

Although employees of defense contractors generally perceived a higher degree of danger from military threats than did their counterparts in the commercial sector, the differences were small. Overall, technology workers in the commercial sector and technology workers at defense contractors agree more than they disagree about the dangers that the United States faces and about when the use of military force would be justified in response to global crises.

Tech workers support the use of military force to defend against foreign aggression: Survey respondents strongly supported using military force to defend the United States and its North Atlantic Treaty Organization (NATO) allies from foreign aggression, with nearly 90 percent of participants finding the use of military force to be justified under these circumstances. A majority of respondents also expressed the belief that the use of military force would be justified to defend foreign nations from attacks by American adversaries in a variety of scenarios. Although a greater percentage of DIB engineers found the use of military force to be justified compared with the other survey populations (Silicon Valley Employees and Alumni of Top CS Universities), the degree of difference was relatively small, and the populations tended to agree more than they disagreed.

However, support across all types of respondents dropped significantly when survey participants were asked their opinion of defending non-NATO allies, such as Saudi Arabia or the Philippines, compared with defending NATO allies under the same circumstances. Potential military conflicts over small islands or other unpopulated territory also drew weaker support, with only one-third of respondents considering the use of military force to be justified under these circumstances. These results could indicate a lower degree of support for the use of military force in response to certain types of crises in the Middle East or East Asia.

Silicon Valley employees have little personal connection to the military: Finally, Silicon Valley Employees had fewer personal ties to the military than did software engineers from the DIB.

- Less than 2 percent of Silicon Valley Employees respondents had ever served in the U.S. armed forces, and more than one-half reported that they did not know anyone close to them who had ever served in the military.
- Respondents from the Silicon Valley Employees population who were veterans of foreign militaries outnumbered U.S. military veterans by nearly 3 to 1.
- In contrast, almost 20 percent of DIB software engineers had previously served in the U.S. military, and only one-quarter of DIB respondents did not have anyone close to them who was either serving or had previously served.

What Do These Findings Mean?

These findings raise some important considerations for DoD. To begin with, the findings demonstrate several areas of potential consensus between DoD and the software engineering community. On the whole, the software engineers surveyed were comfortable deploying AI for a wide variety of military uses, agreed that China and Russia pose a significant threat to the United States, and believed that the use of military force can be justified to combat aggressive actions taken by U.S. adversaries. At the same time, respondents had relatively low levels of trust in the U.S. government and military, and relatively few software engineers who did not already work for defense contractors had any personal experience with or connection to the military. Consequently, the findings suggest areas in which there might be misunderstandings between DoD and the software engineering community and where the two groups might find common ground.

Future Opportunities and Areas for Further Investigation

The survey was designed to understand similarities and differences in attitudes among and between populations—therefore, it should not be used to extrapolate benefits, costs, or risks of current or any alternative DoD strategy or policy. Nonetheless, the results of the survey suggest potential areas to explore for strengthening DoD's relationship with experts and leading high-tech companies that are not traditionally part of the DIB:

- Exploring mechanisms to expand collaborations between DoD and Silicon Valley companies regarding threats posed by cyberattacks, a potential application for AI that Silicon Valley engineers see as a critical global threat.
- Assessing whether expanding engagements among personnel involved with military operations, DoD technical experts, and Silicon Valley individual contributors (nonmanagerial employees) working in technical roles might provide a conduit for developing greater trust between the organizations.
- Exploring the potential benefits of DoD engaging Silicon Valley engineers on some of the details of how DoD intends to use AI and how the military is considering the nuanced and complex situations in which AI would be used. This shared understanding could potentially prevent misinformation or mis-

conceptions on the part of technical experts and reassure the community that DoD is working through how AI-enabled technologies can be used ethically and responsibly.

- Investigating the value of establishing opportunities for DoD and Silicon Valley employees to engage over shared values and principles and the potential benefits of doing so. The recently published DoD ethical principles for AI demonstrate that DoD itself is uncomfortable with some potential uses for AI: This could serve as the foundation for a conversation with Silicon Valley engineers about what AI should and should not be used for.

- Finally, the findings from this survey show that software engineers working for cutting-edge AI firms have few connections to the military experience. Most have little understanding of the operational routines of the military, whether in wartime or in peacetime, and the opportunities that they might have to make a meaningful impact on the daily lives of service members. Thus, another potentially fruitful area for investigation would be assessing the benefits and adapting various types of engagements to help our nation's most innovative and experienced AI experts learn how DoD accomplishes its mission and discover how their talents and expertise can contribute to solving DoD's and the nation's problems.

Contents

Figures

Tables

CHAPTER ONE

Background

Rising Military Capabilities and the Erosion of U.S. Technical Dominance

Since the end of the Cold War, much of the U.S population has taken the technological superiority of the U.S. military as a given.[1] However, technical advances by China and Russia since the beginning of the 21st century may be calling that viewpoint into question, and many military experts believe that foreign forces now pose a credible threat to the U.S. military.[2] As the 2018 National Defense Strategy recognizes, "we are emerging from a period of strategic atrophy, aware that our competitive military advantage has been eroding."[3] Some experts have expressed the belief that artificial intelligence (AI),[4] if exploited to its fullest potential, might become the decisive element in maintaining the United States' military superiority—or in ceding it to a more innovative competitor. Yet others express concerns about the ability of the United States to win this essential race. The final report from the National Security Commission on Artificial Intelligence warns that "China possesses the might, talent, and ambition to surpass the United States as the world's leader in AI" and observes that China has already developed the world's most-advanced AI applications in some areas.[5] In response, the commission argues that the United States should increase its investments in AI and do more to increase the availability of AI talent to ensure that it wins this crucial race.

Private Sector Talent as a Key Resource

If the U.S. Department of Defense (DoD) desires to transform itself through AI, it faces one particularly difficult obstacle. Unlike previous eras of military competition, the private sector now significantly outstrips

---

[1] Chris Dougherty, "Why America Needs a New Way of War," Center for New American Security, June 12, 2019.

[2] Elbridge Colby and David Ochmanek, "How the United States Could Lose a Great-Power War," *RAND Blog*, October 30, 2019; David A. Shlapak and Michael Johnson, *Reinforcing Deterrence on NATO's Eastern Flank: Wargaming the Defense of the Baltics*, Santa Monica, Calif.: RAND Corporation, RR-1253-A, 2016.

[3] James Mattis, *Summary of the 2018 National Defense Strategy of the United States of America*, Washington, D.C.: U.S. Department of Defense, 2018.

[4] *Artificial intelligence* is a term that is notoriously difficult to define. Many studies on the subject choose to explain why offering a definition of the term is so difficult rather than offering a definition of their own. Consequently, the project team has specifically focused this report on the types of applications AI should be used for as opposed to discussing the specifics of how the AI itself works. This should make the findings more enduring as different types of AI approaches are discovered and perfected.

[5] National Security Commission on Artificial Intelligence, *Final Report of the National Security Commission on Artificial Intelligence*, Arlington, Va., March 2021.

the federal government in research and development (R&D) spending.[6] This gap is particularly pronounced in lucrative digital technologies, such as AI. As a direct result, most of the major recent breakthroughs in AI have been achieved by U.S. software companies that focus on private sector customers. Defense contracts account for a slim proportion of their overall business, and even less of this work involves creating solutions custom tailored for government clients.[7] These top companies compete intensely to attract the best talent available, offering lucrative salaries, advanced technical toolsets, and a workplace culture with less formal process and bureaucracy than is found in a typical government agency or government contractor.[8] At the same time, the defense industrial base (DIB) increasingly consists of a relatively small number of companies that specialize in serving the defense industry. Although these companies have a long history of incremental improvements to existing weapon systems and defense capabilities, they do not have the same experience with aggressively pursuing risky investments into unproven or unfamiliar technologies.[9] Consequently, if DoD wants to maintain access to the companies that have the most experience deploying AI solutions and the technical experts at the cutting edge of AI research, it will likely need to collaborate with companies that do not think of themselves as defense contractors.

Purpose of This Study

The purpose of this study is to explore the opinions of software engineers and other technology workers about ways that DoD might use AI to improve its operations. To do so, a RAND research team conducted a large-scale survey from December 2020 through April 2021[10] of nearly 1,200 respondents who are employed by large Silicon Valley corporations, who graduated from top-ranked computer science (CS) programs, or who are employed to build software at companies that are defense contractors. In this report, we examine specific military AI applications and the extent to which respondents felt comfortable or uncomfortable with those applications. It also explores factors that might shape individuals' perceptions of DoD's need to use AI and what are considered to be justifiable uses of military force.

Organization of This Report

The remainder of this report is organized as follows. Chapter Two describes how the research team developed the survey instrument and defines the populations from which the project sought input, the survey recruit-

---

[6] John Sargent and Marcy Gallo, *The Global Research and Development Landscape and Implications for the Department of Defense*, Washington, D.C.: Congressional Research Service, R45403, June 28, 2021.

[7] The commercial market for AI is estimated at $327.5 billion, compared with an estimated $1.4 billion in AI spending by the Defense Department. This estimate does not include money that companies spend on internal investments in AI or money that corporations spend on mergers and acquisitions to acquire AI companies, which would further increase the disparity (see IDC, "IDC Forecasts Improved Growth for Global AI Market in 2021," Needham, Mass., press release, February 23, 2021; and Justin Doubleday, "New Analysis Finds Pentagon Annual Spending on AI Contracts Has Grown to $1.4B," *Inside Defense*, September 24, 2020).

[8] Cade Metz, "Tech Giants Are Paying Huge Salaries for Scarce AI Talent," *New York Times*, October 22, 2017.

[9] Susanna Blume and Molly Parrish, *Make Good Choices, DoD*, Washington, D.C.: Center for a New American Security, November 20, 2019.

[10] As with any survey, real-world events that occurred during the sample period have the potential to affect its results. The research team avoided fielding the survey during the presidential election of 2020 in an attempt to avoid affecting the survey results; however, significant events still occurred during the survey period. The most impactful of these are noted in the analysis.

ment method, and the overall response rates across the different populations. Chapter Three briefly describes the administration of the survey and characteristics of the respondents. Chapter Four reviews the responses to the survey and describes the results. Chapter Five summarizes the key findings from this analysis. Chapter Six discusses potential opportunities for further engagement with Silicon Valley for DoD to consider. Appendix A includes a detailed description of the method for defining and collecting input from the survey respondents and the methods for data analysis. Appendix B is the complete survey instrument, and Appendix C is the survey questions with the aggregated survey responses.

CHAPTER TWO

Survey Design and Survey Populations

This chapter and Chapter Three briefly describe the methods and rationale used to design the survey, recruit participants, administer the survey, and tabulate and analyze the survey responses. Appendix A provides a complete description of the research processes.

Survey Design and Research Questions

The survey instrument was developed using input from subject-matter experts and RAND staff and was informed by other similar survey instruments. An initial draft of the survey instrument was pilot tested with individuals who met the survey selection criteria (as described below in the discussion of survey populations). The team then conducted follow-up interviews with the pilot testers to explore how they had interpreted the survey questions and whether any of the survey questions had been confusing or ambiguous for them. The complete survey instrument appears in Appendix B. Aggregated survey results are provided in Appendix C. The following sections identify the five major topics of inquiry for the study and the research questions that the study sought to investigate within each section.

Military Applications for Artificial Intelligence

The research team addressed two research questions in this section of the survey:

- What factors influence how comfortable and uncomfortable software engineers feel with potential applications of AI for the U.S. military?
- Do software engineers working in the commercial sector significantly differ from software engineers who work for defense contractors in what kinds of military applications for AI make them uncomfortable? If so, what factors correlate with any divergence?

The focus of this study was to investigate and to quantify the kinds of concerns employees (primarily software engineers) of major technology corporations and other software engineers in the private sector might have about contributing to AI-enabled capabilities used by DoD. This is a complicated and nuanced topic. To explore the variety of views that software engineers might have when considering working on a project for DoD, the research team engaged in a structured brainstorming exercise on possible military application of AI and then designed a survey that presented respondents with the resulting 13 hypothetical applications in the form of scenarios (one question was posed about each scenario; see Appendix B). These scenarios ranged from using AI to control lethal activities on the battlefield to back-office activities far removed from any potential use of force (such as "Using AI to audit the U.S. military's financial transactions"). The research team hypothesized that respondents would establish a clear ordering of these scenarios, with some of the scenarios seen as more acceptable for the military to undertake and others seen as less acceptable.

The research team hypothesized that two characteristics (factors) would correlate with a respondent's comfort level. First, they hypothesized that survey respondents would be less comfortable with activities that had a greater destructive effect than with activities that had a protective effect. In some scenarios, the survey put these two characteristics in tension to explore which would be more compelling. For example, one question asked respondents how comfortable they would feel about "using artificial intelligence to reduce civilian casualties and collateral damage to humanitarian targets, such as hospitals by more precisely targeting enemy soldiers." The research team expected that most respondents would see the reduction of harm to civilians and other innocent bystanders as a good, but that some portion of respondents would be reluctant to use AI to assist in activities that would harm human beings—even if those individuals are enemy soldiers.

The second characteristic (factor) about which the researchers hypothesized and that the survey varied across the question set involved the relative distance of the AI algorithm from the battlefield. The research team hypothesized that survey respondents would be less comfortable with AI applications deployed on the battlefield compared with AI applications that either supported battlefield operations but did not actually operate on the battlefield (such as logistics and supply-chain management) or were deployed to improve DoD's back-office functions (such as auditing financial transactions).

Two Special Cases

The survey also included two scenarios designed to differentiate between two possible types of objections to helping DoD build AI applications.

First, the survey included a scenario that asked whether the respondent would be willing to build AI to help a nongovernmental organization (NGO) respond to natural disasters. This scenario was intended to identify individuals who would not feel comfortable assisting DoD with any type of AI application but would feel comfortable building AI applications for other organizations.

The second scenario asked whether the respondent would feel comfortable helping DoD prevent the use of AI by other militaries in a way that would not require the respondent to build an AI algorithm for DoD itself. This scenario was intended to quantify the number of individuals who are concerned about the long-term development of AI and believe that the technology itself is too dangerous for humanity to develop.[1] The reason that these individuals would not feel comfortable developing AI algorithms for DoD is that they object to improving AI, not that they object to DoD's mission.

"Should AI Work?" Versus "Can AI Work?"

One important instruction provided to the survey respondents as they considered each hypothetical scenario was to assume "that the AI works and achieves the intended goal." In reality, this is a bold statement. AI algorithms do not always provide the improvements that their developers promise, and some fall far short of their intended purpose. Engineers, in particular, may have good reason to be skeptical of the claims made about a technology; they are more aware than anyone else of the bugs and imperfections that nearly every piece of software includes.

However, the purpose of this survey was not to determine whether the respondents believe that AI can provide benefits on the battlefield. Rather, it was to determine whether software engineers and others working for companies developing advanced AI algorithms object to the very idea that AI algorithms should ever be developed to benefit DoD. These two concerns are of a very different nature. Unresolved concerns and questions surround the verification, validation, test, and evaluation (VVT&E) of AI algorithms and whether the behavior of AI algorithms can be retroactively explained (explainable AI). Resolving these concerns, or determining that no adequate resolution exists, is a technical matter that experts can discuss and debate. In

---

[1] Kelsey Piper, "The Case for Taking AI Seriously as a Threat to Humanity," *Vox*, October 15, 2020.

contrast, disagreements over the mission and purpose of DoD are not technical in nature: They represent differences in ethical principles, world view, and philosophy. Both topics are worthy of study, but this project focuses only on the latter considerations.

Survey Instrument Language

Finally, when designing the questions for the survey, the RAND research team focused on ensuring that they would be clear and understandable to survey participants who would not necessarily have any personal familiarity with military operations, jargon, terminology, or policies. Consequently, the questions used less-formal, more-colloquial descriptions for the different potential applications for AI instead of terminology used in official U.S. government or DoD policies. As a result, the applications of AI described in the survey should not be interpreted as reflections of current DoD policies or potential policy options regarding the use of AI, or autonomy, or autonomous systems. Instead, the survey results clarify some of the factors that the software engineers who will have to implement these applications are taking into consideration when they approach these issues.

Trust in Institutions and Individuals

This section of the survey focused on three overarching research questions:

- Is there a correlation between the degree of trust that software engineers have in societal institutions—specifically, in DoD—and their perception of the acceptability of building AI applications for DoD?
- How do perceptions shift in discussions of trust in societal institutions as compared with discussions of trust in the individuals who belong to an institution?
- Who has credibility within the software engineering community?

One factor that might explain the willingness or unwillingness of individuals to assist DoD is the degree of trust that those individuals have in the U.S. government as a whole and in DoD specifically. Trust in many of the major institutions in U.S life has declined markedly in the post–Vietnam era. For example, a survey conducted in 2021 found that only 24 percent of Americans felt that they could trust the government to do what is right, down from 77 percent in 1964.[2] Recent surveys of the U.S. public have found the military to be an exception to this phenomenon, with 72 percent of Americans reporting that they felt "a great deal" or "quite a lot" of trust in the military in 2020.[3] However, it has been unclear whether AI experts also trust the military more than other institutions in society.

Two sections of the survey explored the degree of trust that the respondents had in the U.S. government and DoD. In one section, the survey asked respondents whether they trust the listed institutions to act in a way that they agree with. The phrasing of the question was intended to prompt the respondent not to passively judge the given options but rather to express their comfort in being a member of that institution and whether they would be prepared to accept a degree of complicity in the behavior of that institution. In addition, a second section of the survey asked about the respondent's degree of trust in various members of the listed institutions. In this way, the survey aimed to distinguish between the degree to which a respondent believes the institution will take actions that they agree with versus their trust that individual members of those institutions will behave in ways they would find acceptable. The survey also inquired about respondents' levels of trust in a variety of roles in DoD and in technology companies, to understand whom software

---

[2] Pew Research Center, "Public Trust in Government: 1958–2021," survey database, May 17, 2021.

[3] Gallup, "Confidence in Institutions," survey database, undated-a.

engineers trust and whom they regard with a greater degree of skepticism. Questions in this portion of the survey were informed by Gallup's *Confidence in Institutions* survey[4] and Pew Research's *Trust and Distrust in America*.[5] The questions use the same response scale as the Gallup surveys. The research team included four of the institutions from the Gallup survey and added several institutions relevant to this project. Similarly, the research team chose four categories of individuals associated with those institutions from the Pew Research surveys and added several categories of individuals that focused on areas relevant to this project.

Perception of Global Threats

This section of the survey included two research questions:

- Do software engineers perceive the countries that DoD has identified as strategic competitors as a meaningful threat to the United States?
- Do software engineers perceive potential military threats as important relative to other types of threats the United States faces?

An additional factor that might explain survey respondents' willingness or unwillingness to assist DoD is how they perceive the potential threats that DoD confronts. Although DoD is naturally focused on foreign adversaries and the ways that those adversaries might attempt to harm American interests or kill American citizens, these are not the only threats that the United States faces. The scenarios were designed to explore a variety of potential threats—including military, financial, and environmental threats—to determine whether respondents believed that non-military threats presented a greater danger to the United States than military threats. This also allowed us to consider whether those opinions correlated with their willingness to work on AI projects for DoD.

Similarly, the 2018 National Defense Strategy named four countries for specific concerns—China, Russia, Iran, and North Korea.[6] Thus, the research team was interested in assessing the survey populations' perception of the potential threat from these countries and their beliefs regarding whether DoD already has comprehensively addressed those threats. Believing that DoD has already addressed the threat might correlate with a lower degree of willingness to help DoD develop AI-enabled capabilities.

Questions used in this portion of the survey were informed by the 2019 Chicago Council Survey[7] and SSRS polling for CNN on international affairs topics.[8] The research team supplemented the list of survey questions and types of global threats with additional topics that were relevant to the project.

Information Sources and Other Influences

This section of the survey addressed two research questions:

---

[4] Gallup, undated-a.

[5] Lee Rainie, Scott Keeter, and Andrew Perrin, *Trust and Distrust in America*, Washington, D.C.: Pew Research Center, July 22, 2019

[6] Mattis, 2018.

[7] Dina Smeltz, Ivo Daalder, Karl Friedhoff, Craig Kafura, and Brendan Helm, *Rejecting Retreat: Results of the 2019 Chicago Council Survey of American Public Opinion and U.S. Foreign Policy*, Chicago: Chicago Council on Global Affairs, September 16, 2019.

[8] SSRS, opinions about Donald Trump, telephone survey conducted for CNN, January 20, 2020.

- What types of news media and other sources of information are software engineers relying on to inform them about events related to DoD?
- What past events have shaped perceptions about how DoD intends to use AI?

The sources of information that individuals rely on can influence their views. In particular, social media can filter or amplify the flow of information presented to an individual. In some cases, information sources can also serve as information bubbles if the people who rely on them use them only to validate pre-existing beliefs and biases.[9] Consequently, the research team wanted to explore what types of information sources the survey respondents relied on to learn about global events and technological advancements. The researchers also investigated the kinds of past events and major news stories that survey respondents reported as having had the greatest influence on their perception of how DoD might use AI in the future.

The survey question about Americans' trust in the news media and the response scale for the frequency with which respondents receive their news from various sources were both taken from Gallup polling about the media.[10]

Justifications for the Use of Military Force

This section of the survey addressed two research questions:

- What factors influence whether software engineers believe that the use of military would be justified?
- What percentage of software engineers believe that military force should not be used under any circumstances?

Finally, as DoD's focus has shifted to preparing for inter-state competition with near-peer competitors,[11] there has been increasing interest in the need to potentially mobilize a greater swath of U.S. society than was required to wage the wars in Afghanistan and Iraq. Conventional wisdom among experienced Silicon Valley entrepreneurs and managers is that software engineering teams are most productive when they believe in their organization's purpose and want to perform to the best of their abilities.[12] Consequently, the degree to which technology workers perceive that a conflict is justified or unjustified could significantly affect the degree of support that DoD would receive from the U.S. technology sector in the event of hostilities with a major adversary.

Survey Populations

When considering potential answers to these research questions, the research team recognized that the population that they wanted to survey—software engineers—is not a monolithic bloc. Instead, many factors may shape the experiences that software engineers have had and thus how they have arrived at their opinions on these critical issues. To capture the widest possible range of views, using the broadest range of backgrounds,

---

[9] Dominic Spohr, "Fake News and Ideological Polarization: Filter Bubbles and Selective Exposure on Social Media," *Business Information Review*, Vol. 34, No. 3, 2017.

[10] Gallup, "Media Use and Evaluation," webpage, undated-b.

[11] Mattis, 2018.

[12] "Mercenaries vs. Missionaries: John Doerr Sees Two Kinds of Internet Entrepreneurs," *Knowledge@Wharton*, blog post, April 13, 2000.

the researchers recruited participants for this survey from three distinct populations. This section describes those populations.

Silicon Valley Employees

First, the team sought to recruit survey participants from the largest software corporations that are typically associated with Silicon Valley. Although they did not limit the recruitment of survey respondents to any one geographical area, the report generally refers to Silicon Valley Employees as working for the large high-tech companies that are (1) at the leading edge of AI R&D and AI-enabled capabilities and products and (2) not traditional defense contractors. In particular, survey recruitment focused on three such companies: Google, Microsoft, and Amazon. Each of these companies pursues the best talent available in the software industry and invests billions of dollars specifically in advancing their ability to implement AI-enhanced algorithms, products, and capabilities.[13] Each company also has developed an advanced cloud computing environment, a key enabler of machine learning (ML) and modern AI development.[14] Finally, each of these companies has, at various points, actively sought to obtain AI or cloud computing contracts from DoD. Although other large Silicon Valley technology companies, such as Facebook and Apple, are also making large investments in AI, they have had less interaction with DoD than have the three companies on which recruitment focused.[15]

For this survey, the researchers sought to capture the views of both technical staff and nontechnical corporate staff of these corporations. Although technical staff are the best placed to implement AI algorithms and build new solutions, nontechnical staff at these companies have access to internal discussion forums and all-hands meetings, where their views can influence the opinions of their technical coworkers. For example, one of the organizers of the Google Walkout, in which 20,000 Google employees worldwide participated in a one-day strike against the company to protest its past handling of sexual harassment cases, was a nontechnical employee in the marketing department.[16]

For the recruitment of Amazon employees, the team did not include staff in warehouse or retail roles, as employees in these roles at Amazon do not seem to have the same degree of influence over technical staff or corporate leadership as their Google counterparts.[17] As discussed in the section of Appendix A focused on sample representativeness, 90 percent of the employees recruited to take the survey had technical roles (e.g., software development, product management, test or quality assurance [QA], and site reliability engineers), and analysis of the responses indicates that the opinions of technical staff and non-technical staff on these topics were similar.

Of note, a significant number of individuals who met these criteria may not be U.S. citizens. The researchers chose not to filter based on citizenship to capture the full spectrum of views held by individuals within this community.

---

[13] Dina Bass and Joshua Brustein, "Big Tech Swallows Most of the Hot AI Startups," *Bloomberg News*, March 16, 2020.

[14] Steve Lohr, "At Tech's Leading Edge, Worry About a Concentration of Power," *New York Times*, September 26, 2019.

[15] Jack Poulson, "Reports of a Silicon Valley/Military Divide Have Been Greatly Exaggerated," *Tech Inquiry*, July 7, 2020.

[16] Nick Statt, "Google Walkout Organizer Claire Stapleton Tells Her Story of the Company's Retaliation," *Wired*, December 12, 2019.

[17] Jodi Kantor, Karen Weise, and Grace Ashford, "Inside Amazon's Employment Machine," *New York Times*, June 15, 2021.

Comparison Groups

To understand how opinions among employees of Silicon Valley corporations might vary relative to the rest of the software engineering community, the researchers selected two groups against which to compare their sample of interest.

Alumni of Top Ranked Computer Science Universities

For the first comparison group, the researchers wanted to consider the possibility that engineers working for the largest software corporations in Silicon Valley might differ from software engineers working in other kinds of firms. To consider this potential variance, the researchers recruited a comparison group (Alumni of Top CS Universities) consisting of individuals who had graduated from a top-ranked CS department[18] with a CS degree but who were not currently working for one of the Silicon Valley corporations.[19] The academic background of these individuals demonstrates that they have the technical capability to create advanced software products and to learn cutting-edge technologies. This group also provides a window into the views of the broader software community and how individuals who work outside the largest and best-funded software companies may view potential military applications of AI.

Just as with the Silicon Valley Employees survey population, a meaningful number of individuals who are not U.S. citizens may have met the criteria for inclusion in this survey population.

In addition, because of limitations in the source data, it is possible that some of the individuals in this group who attended multiple universities may have received a non-CS degree from one of the listed schools and a CS degree from a university not included on this list.

Defense Industrial Base

The second comparison group, DIB, included software engineers who work for companies for whom DoD is a significant portion of their business. Examples include Lockheed Martin, Northrop Grumman, Boeing, and Raytheon. Unlike employees of the technology giants of Silicon Valley, software engineers at these companies routinely conduct work for DoD. Consequently, their technical employees represent a mix of influences. On the one hand, their training and education has been similar to that of their counterparts in large technology companies, and they share many of the same day-to-day responsibilities and activities. On the other hand, individuals who have chosen to accept employment with these companies are, we assume, aware that DoD is a significant if not the primary customer for many of their employer's products and services. Thus, comparing the views of these individuals with those of their counterparts at the largest technology companies should shed light on the degree to which their life experiences have resulted in similar or divergent opinions.

Literature Review of Other Surveys

Several previous studies have sought to investigate various aspects of how the U.S. general public or AI experts view ethics and governance questions involving potential military uses for AI. The researchers conducted a

---

[18] We defined *top-ranked computer science departments* as the top ten schools from *U.S. News and World Report*'s 2019 ranking of the best undergraduate CS programs ("Best Global Universities for Computer Science in the United States," *U.S. News and World Report*, 2019).

[19] We attempted to exclude any individuals who would qualify for inclusion in the other two survey populations (Silicon Valley Employees and DIB) from being recruited in the Alumni of Top CS Universities population. A review of the current employer for all of the survey respondents indicates that three respondents worked for an independently run subsidiary corporation of the three Silicon Valley corporations and three worked for a defense contractor (out of a total of 252 respondents). The rest worked for a wide variety of universities, nonprofits, and private sector companies of all sizes and industries.

brief review of these studies and summarize the differences between their approach and the approach taken by this project.

Three studies have surveyed individuals about their attitudes toward military uses for AI. The first, published in the *Journal of Artificial Intelligence Research*, surveyed 524 AI/ML researchers from China, Europe, and the United States about three potential military uses for AI (e.g., lethal autonomous weapons, surveillance, and logistics) and about which organizations they trusted the most to develop AI in the public's interest.[20] It found that respondents supported logistics applications for AI but opposed lethal autonomous weapons and surveillance applications for AI. It also showed that AI/ML researchers trusted international organizations and NGOs the most to develop AI in the public interest. The second, conducted by the Center for Security and Emerging Technology (CSET), surveyed 160 AI experts regarding the reasons they would or would not wish to work on DoD-funded AI projects.[21] It found that only 38 percent of its respondents felt positively about the possibility of working on DoD-funded AI projects, against 22 percent who felt negatively and 40 percent who were neutral about the prospect. The CSET survey also found stronger support for back-office or humanitarian applications of AI compared with battlefield applications for the technology. Finally, a third study by the Centre for the Governance of AI surveyed 2,000 members of the U.S. general public about which societal institutions they trusted the most to develop AI in the interest of the public.[22] This survey found that members of the U.S. public trusted the U.S. military and university researchers the most to develop AI in the public interest.

The current study differs from these prior surveys in several ways. First, this study has a substantially larger sample size (1,178) than did previous efforts to survey technical experts on this topic. Second, the current survey expands its focus to include not only researchers but also software engineers and other technical staff involved in designing, implementing, and deploying AI/ML applications. Third, this survey is the only one to include software engineers working for defense contractors as a distinct comparison group. Finally, this survey both focuses on a broader range of topics and explores each of those topics in greater detail than did these other efforts. The strengths of the current study will improve the ability to understand the nuances and specifics of these important issues.

---

[20] Baobao Zhang, Markus Anderljung, Lauren Kahn, Noemi Dreksler, Michael Horowitz, and Allan Dafoe, "Ethics and Governance of Artificial Intelligence: Evidence from a Survey of Machine Learning Researchers," *Journal of Artificial Intelligence Research*, Vol. 71, 2021.

[21] Catherine Aiken, Rebecca Kagan, and Michael Page, "'Cool Projects' or 'Expanding the Efficiency of the Murderous American War Machine?'" Center for Security and Emerging Technology, issue brief, November 2020.

[22] Baobao Zhang and Allan Dafoe, "U.S. Public Opinion on the Governance of Artificial Intelligence," New York: *Proceedings of the AAAI/ACM Conference on AI, Ethics, and Society*, February 2020.

CHAPTER THREE

Survey Execution

Survey Administration

This survey was fielded in a web-based format between December 9, 2020, and April 30, 2021, by the RAND Survey Research Group. Sampled individuals were contacted no more than four times (an initial outreach email and up to three follow-up emails requesting participation). Emails were discontinued either when the individual completed the survey or when they asked not to be contacted further. The survey required approximately 15 minutes to complete. All respondents completed the same survey instrument; however, the ordering of questions within the sections of the survey was randomized across participants to reduce the potential for a skewed result.

RAND's Institutional Review Board reviewed and approved the study procedures and survey instrument to ensure that it met all human subjects protection protocols. The Human Subjects Protection Committee conducted second-level review of human subjects protections. The study procedures, or portions of them, also received reviews and approvals by DoD's Office of People Analytics; the Office of Information Management; the Records, Privacy, and Declassification Division; and the Defense Privacy, Civil Liberties, and Transparency Division.

Recruitment

To recruit survey participants from the target populations of interest, the research team employed three techniques. First, they purchased email addresses from commercial providers to draw random samples of email addresses of eligible individuals to invite via email. Second, the researchers placed targeted advertisements on LinkedIn.com to allow individuals who met the study eligibility criteria to opt into the study and complete the survey. Third, the researchers invited employees of Northrop Grumman who were enrolled in their AI Academy to take the survey. Ultimately, most survey participants were recruited through email invitations; only approximately 2 percent of participants were recruited through the other two means. No financial incentives were offered for survey completion.

Using these three methods, the researchers recruited a total of 1,198 individuals to complete the survey. Table 3.1 displays the number of recruitment emails sent, by population, and the overall response rate. Response rates for the Silicon Valley Employees and DIB populations were lower than expected, most likely because the survey invitations were sometimes marked as spam emails as the survey progressed.[1] These response rates reflect the general trend of low response rates across survey modes, especially with online

---

[1] Response rates for the alumni of top CS universities population were not affected by this issue because this population was recruited last, and by that point in survey execution, the study team had adapted its email invitation processes to avoid inclusion in the spam filters.

TABLE 3.1
Response Rates, by Population

Population Name	Invitations Sent	Number of Responses	Response Rate (%)
Silicon Valley Employees	78,093	742	0.95
Defense Industrial Base	20,323	204	1.0
Alumni of Top CS Universities	9,558	252	2.64
Total	107,974	1,198	1.11

recruitment of hard-to-reach and hidden populations lacking a representative sampling frame.[2] The most directly comparable survey, conducted among U.S. AI experts by CSET in 2020, had a 4-percent response rate for the short version of its survey instrument and a 1.6-percent response rate for the long version of its survey instrument.[3] Finally, low response rates alone do not necessarily suggest nonresponse bias. According to Krosnick, 1999, and Dillman, 1991, when respondent characteristics are equally representative of nonrespondents, low rates of return are not biasing. The research team analyzed sample representativeness to provide insights about the generalizability of survey estimates. The results of that analysis are described in the "Sample Size and Precision" section of Appendix A. Recruiting adequate sample sizes for each of the target populations allowed us to obtain stable estimates with reasonable precision for each population.

Data Cleaning and Data Quality

The research team carefully inspected the survey data to identify responses that did not appear to be a good faith attempt to answer the survey questions accurately. Three criteria were used to select potentially invalid responses. First, multiple choice answers were scanned to look for long streaks of identical answers—defined as greater than 20 identical (consecutive) multiple choice answers in a row. Second, multiple choice answers were scanned to look for especially short streaks of identical answers—an average streak length of 1.1 or less. Finally, the open-ended question responses were manually reviewed to determine whether the answer given was at all responsive to the initial prompt. These three factors were considered together when determining whether a completed survey was valid, with the responses to the open-ended questions given the most weight when assessing validity. Only 20 surveys were determined to be invalid and removed from data analysis based on these criteria. Table 3.2 shows the response rates by category of survey respondents and final response status (full complete, partial complete, or invalid survey). *Complete surveys* are defined as those for which respondents read through the entire survey and did not abandon it. Although some respondents may have chosen not to answer a handful of questions, individuals who completed the survey generally answered all or nearly all the questions. *Partial completes* are defined as those in which the survey respondent exited the survey before reaching the final question. Among those who were recruited and started a survey, most completed a survey and their responses (or data) are of good quality.

---

[2] Weimiao Fan and Zheng Yan, "Factors Affecting Response Rates of the Web Survey: A Systematic Review," *Computers in Human Behavior*, Vol. 26, No. 2, 2010.

[3] Aiken, Kagan, and Page, 2020.

TABLE 3.2
Completed Surveys, by Population

Population Name	Partially Completed Surveys	Completed Surveys	Invalid Surveys	Number of Valid Surveys
Silicon Valley Employees	93	633	16	726
Defense Industrial Base	22	178	4	200
Alumni of Top CS Universities	29	223	0	252

Events that Occurred During the Survey Data Collection Period

Any real-world events that occur while a survey is in the field have the potential to affect the results. On the one hand, recent events might seem more prominent to a respondent than do other impactful events that may have occurred at some point in the more distant past. On the other hand, some survey participants will not have the opportunity to react to events that occur during the survey data collection period but that happen after those participants had completed the survey. Figure 3.1 presents some of the most-significant events that occurred during the survey period. Two of these events—the SolarWinds cyber breach and the attack on the U.S. Capitol building—were mentioned by multiple survey respondents in their responses to open-ended questions on the survey asking about what types of real-world events had affected their views about how DoD might use AI and whether they believed it would use AI responsibly in the future.

FIGURE 3.1
Time Line of Major Events During the Survey Data Collection

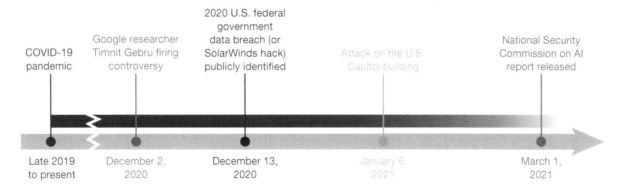

15

CHAPTER FOUR

Survey Results and Analysis

This chapter presents the findings of the survey, followed by analyses of demographic and other factors among the survey respondents that reveal some potential associations. The first five sections in this chapter describe the results of each of the five sections of the survey, as described in Chapter Two:

- "Military Applications for AI"
- "Trust in Institutions and Individuals"
- "Perception of Global Threat"
- "Information Sources and Other Influences"
- "Justifications for the Use of Military Force."

The remaining sections of this chapter describe the results of the analyses to assess the potential association of population group, demographic factors, and other characteristics in participants' survey responses.

Military Applications for Artificial Intelligence

The first section of the survey asked respondents to indicate their comfort levels in employing AI for a variety of military purposes, as illustrated with brief scenarios. Each scenario was written using common terms and phrases for clarity and to ensure that each scenario was distinct from others. Respondents were asked to select one of five responses: very comfortable, somewhat comfortable, neutral, somewhat uncomfortable, and very uncomfortable. Respondents also had the choice to skip answering questions for any of the scenarios.

Analysis of the survey responses reveals that the scenarios can be split into three groupings based on similar responses:

- The first grouping includes scenarios in which AI can use lethal force without approval from a human being (human out-of-the-loop, that is, unsupervised).
- The second grouping includes scenarios in which AI will recommend uses of military force that could have lethal consequences, but where a human makes the final decision (human in-the-loop). The wording for two questions in the second grouping is ambiguous as to whether the use of force is supervised or unsupervised; these will be discussed below.
- The third grouping includes scenarios that do not involve the use of lethal force by AI. These scenarios involve the use of AI in activities that either occur off of the battlefield or protect service members on the battlefield without harming other humans.

Finally, two special cases that either do not involve DoD or do not involve the use of AI will be considered separately.

One important factor to note is that the scenarios were not written to correspond with actual or desired military uses for AI or with U.S. government and DoD policies. The use of AI for battlefield and nonbattlefield scenarios is a complex topic with a wide variety of complicating factors. It would be impossible to exhaustively consider all of these nuances and describe them to an audience unfamiliar with military operations in any survey instrument. Instead, these scenarios were designed to explore how software engineers in the private sector—who would not be expected to be familiar with military jargon or have ever read a government policy document—thought about these kinds of issues. The survey was designed to understand similarities and differences in attitudes among and between populations, and it should not be used to extrapolate benefits, costs, or risks of current or any alternative DoD strategy or policy.

In several cases, questions were designed to operate as pairs to test whether slightly changing the scenario led to a meaningful change in the answers from the respondents. For example, one question asked about optimizing the supply chain to bring "food, medical supplies, and fuel" to the battlefield, while a second asked about bringing "weapons, ammunition, and spare parts" instead. These variations in the question prompt were intended to identify which specific factors correlate with the greatest increases and decreases in the overall comfort of the survey respondents and reveal areas with a greater or lesser degree of consensus among the surveyed populations.

Unsupervised Use of Lethal Force by Artificial Intelligence

The scenarios in this first group would allow an AI algorithm to use lethal force against human targets without human supervision. Figure 4.1 shows the relative comfort and discomfort levels that respondents felt about these options:

As the figure illustrates, a significantly larger percentage of respondents from each surveyed population indicated that they were either somewhat or very uncomfortable with granting an AI the ability to potentially kill humans without human supervision than was the percentage that indicated that they were comfortable with this power (top panel). Although software engineers working for DIB contractors were more likely to feel comfortable with these scenarios than were Silicon Valley Employees or Alumni of Top CS Universities respondents, a majority of individuals even in the DIB population are opposed to granting AI this power. Noting that employing AI in this way could save the lives of U.S. service members had a minimal effect on the comfort level of the Silicon Valley Employees and Alumni of Top CS Universities populations (4 percent

FIGURE 4.1

Unsupervised Use of Lethal Force by Artificial Intelligence

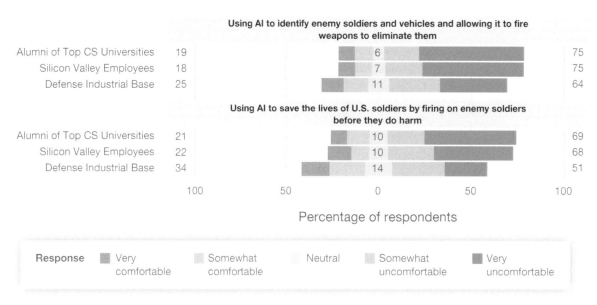

more and 2 percent more of each population, respectively) (lower panel). Although an additional 9 percent of the DIB population was comfortable with AI that can act quickly enough to protect U.S. service members, a slight majority (51 percent) remained uncomfortable with the potential that AI without supervision could harm humans.

The researcher team conducted regression analysis to determine whether these differences between populations were statistically significant and were not simply the result of demographic differences across populations (e.g., the DIB population was older than the other two). The regressions found that the difference between Alumni of Top CS Universities and DIB was statistically significant at the alpha = .05 level for both questions, while the difference between Silicon Valley Employees and DIB was significant only for the latter question ("using AI to save the lives of U.S. soldiers . . . ").

Other Use of Lethal Force by Artificial Intelligence

The second grouping of questions involves scenarios that either state or imply that AI algorithms will play a role in allowing the military to use lethal force against humans (Figure 4.2).

Two of these scenarios specify that AI will lack the ability to use lethal force itself but instead will only make recommendations or provide data to inform decisions ultimately made by military personnel (the first and third panels in Figure 4.2).

FIGURE 4.2

Supervised Use of Lethal Force by Artificial Intelligence

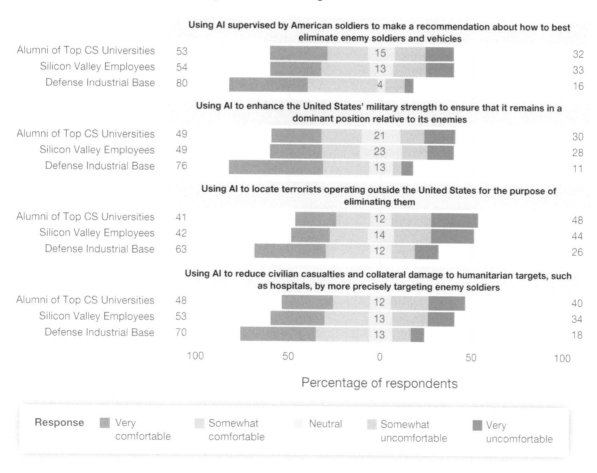

The other two scenarios do not clearly specify the degree of control that humans will have over the use of lethal force. One of the two scenarios (panel 2 in Figure 4.2) asked whether respondents would be comfortable "using AI to enhance the United States' military strength to ensure it remains in a dominant position relative to its enemies." The scenario does not clearly state that this will involve the use of lethal force or the exact types of weapons or military operations that AI would enable. However, the variety of responses for this scenario were similar to those for the questions specifying that AI would be used to recommend lethal actions to U.S. service members. Moreover, the responses to this question were unlike the responses to the question specifying that AI would be given independent (unsupervised) control over lethal actions itself (Figure 4.1). Consequently, it is likely that most survey respondents interpreted this question to imply that AI would be used to enhance weapon systems or use lethal force under the supervision of U.S. service members and that it did not imply the creation of autonomous lethal weapon systems.

Finally, the fourth scenario asked respondents to rate their comfort level with an AI that "reduces civilian casualties and collateral damage to humanitarian targets, such as hospitals, by more precisely targeting enemy soldiers." However, the question did not clearly specify whether the AI is under the control of human service members or whether AI can act autonomously. Some respondents might have interpreted the question as allowing AI to act only under human supervision: If so, this would explain the relative similarity of the responses to this scenario with those for the other two scenarios that clearly state that AI will only recommend potentially lethal actions to U.S. service members. Alternatively, it is also possible that some survey respondents placed a high value on the lives of noncombatants and would be willing to allow more autonomous AIs if they successfully reduce the human cost of war.

As these results demonstrate, there is a significant split among the three populations over their comfort level with these scenarios. Silicon Valley Employees and Alumni of Top CS Universities respondents expressed mixed reactions about whether these types of applications for AI are acceptable.

Respondents were most evenly split about potentially using AI to support the Global War on Terror (Panel 3 in Figure 4.2). Silicon Valley Employees respondents were divided evenly between those who were comfortable and those who were uncomfortable with using AI to locate terrorists overseas, while a slight plurality of Alumni of Top CS Universities participants expressed discomfort with the potential use of AI for this purpose.

Respondents from the Silicon Valley Employees and the Alumni of Top CS Universities populations expressed greater comfort levels with the three remaining uses of AI (Panels 1, 2, and 4). However, nearly one-third of the respondents indicated that they were uncomfortable with all three of these uses of AI.

In contrast, a larger proportion of respondents from the DIB expressed comfort with all four of these uses of AI, compared with the other two population groups. Although locating potential terrorists also draws the greatest degree of opposition from the DIB among the four scenarios, a clear majority of respondents are comfortable with all four of the hypothetical scenarios, with as little as 11 percent of respondents expressing discomfort with using AI to ensure that the U.S. military remains in a dominant position over its opponents. This split among the three populations may be unsurprising, but the variance is particularly notable because opinions elicited by the other scenarios do not show the same degree of difference among the survey populations. It also gives an indication of the relative shift among the populations for these types of questions.

For all of four of these questions, population was a statistically significant driver of the differences in survey responses at the alpha = 0.5 level. Population was a statistically significant driver of differences in response for every question in this subset of scenarios. Moreover, the population variable's T-values—the measure of their significance—were among the highest of all the questions. Of the eight coefficients (one for each population across four questions), seven were significant at the alpha = 0.1 level. Furthermore, the coefficients for populations were among the highest for these questions. This latter finding indicates that, compared with factors associated with differences in responses to other survey questions, population was more relevant to survey responses for these questions. For the Alumni of Top CS Universities variable, these questions' coefficients ranked 1st, 4th, 7th, and 14th out of all 59 multiple-choice questions in the survey. For the Silicon Valley Employees population, the ranks were 1st, 5th, 9th, and 21st. The question "Using AI to enhance the United States' military strength to ensure it remains in a dominant position relative to its enemies" had the largest coefficient of all the questions asked in the survey for both the Alumni of Top CS Universities and Silicon Valley Employees variables.

Protective and Nonbattlefield Uses for Artificial Intelligence

The questions in the last grouping do not involve the direct use of lethal force under the direction of AI algorithms. These questions involve either the use of AI on the battlefield in a way that would not involve potentially harming humans or uses of AI by the military off of the battlefield. Figure 4.3 displays these results.

Respondents in all of the surveyed populations were overwhelmingly comfortable with these potential uses of AI. For each scenario, at least three-quarters of respondents indicated that they were very comfortable or somewhat comfortable with the proposed use of AI. Interestingly, indirectly enabling lethal activities— for example, bringing ammunition and spare parts for vehicles to the battlefield—resulted in only about a

FIGURE 4.3
Protective and Nonbattlefield Uses for Artificial Intelligence

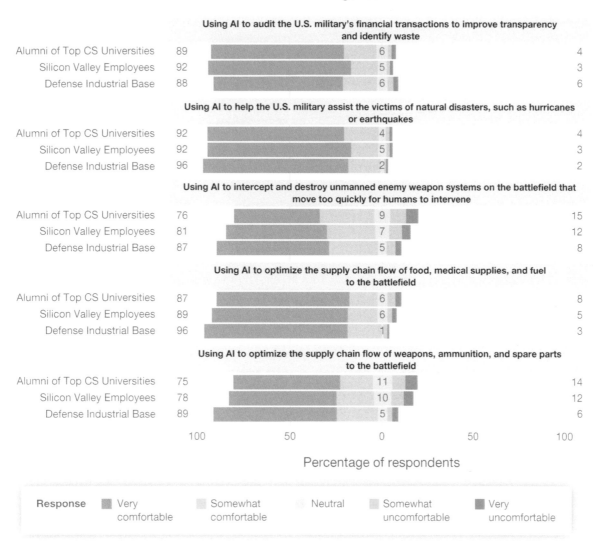

10-percentage-point decrease in respondent comfort levels with the activity compared with similar activities that were farther removed from enabling combat operations (e.g., bringing food, medical supplies, and fuel to the battlefield). Although respondents displayed the most comfort with enabling humanitarian operations, the data show that the other potential applications of AI summarized in Figure 4.3 would be relatively uncontroversial within the Silicon Valley Employees and Alumni of Top CS Universities populations.

For three of these questions, the Alumni of Top CS Universities population had statistically significant differences in their responses; however, no statistically significant differences were seen between the responses of the Silicon Valley Employees and DIB populations for any of these questions.

In addition to population, gender and age were often statistically significant factors contributing to the differences in attitudes. This was true across all the scenarios covered in Figures 4.1, 4.2, and 4.3. Women were typically less comfortable than were men with the AI scenarios, especially those that involved lethal force. Older respondents were more comfortable with AI scenarios than were younger ones. Thus, even when differences in demographics can explain some of the difference between populations, membership in a particular population (i.e., Silicon Valley Employees, Alumni of Top CS Universities, DIB) alone remains a statistically significant factor. The other variables—connection to the military, years of experience working in the industry, or state of residence—were rarely significantly associated with differences in attitudes.

Two Special Cases

Finally, the questions included two special cases that did not involve the use of AI by DoD. The first question replaced DoD with a humanitarian NGO that intended to use AI to assist the victims of natural disasters. The second asked respondents to assess their comfort level in potentially helping DoD prevent the use of AI by enemy militaries in ways that did not require DoD to use AI itself. These questions allowed the research team to identify and quantify two types of respondents. Respondents who are comfortable with the use of AI by an NGO but uncomfortable or neutral in response to all of the scenarios involving DoD are considered to be uncomfortable with DoD's use of AI. In contrast, respondents who are comfortable with preventing the use of AI by enemy militaries but uncomfortable with or neutral toward all of the scenarios involving the use of AI, even by a humanitarian NGO, are considered to be uncomfortable with the further development of AI. Although it may seem paradoxical for members of these survey populations to be uncomfortable with AI itself, some prominent technology experts have expressed concerns that AI could ultimately have a negative effect on humanity or even, in the worst case, threaten its very existence.[1] This viewpoint should not be mistaken for discomfort with DoD; in fact, individuals with these views might be especially motivated to assist DoD with preventing foreign governments from developing and deploying their own AI algorithms for military purposes.

The data indicate that each of these two populations comprises a small percentage of the surveyed population overall. A total of ten respondents out of 1,178 (five from the Silicon Valley Employees population and five from the Alumni of Top CS Universities population) expressed discomfort with all of the hypothetical military uses for AI and with any action by DoD to prevent hostile militaries deploying AI applications for their own purposes (indicating discomfort with DoD). A total of seven respondents (four from the Silicon Valley Employees population, one from the Alumni of Top CS Universities population, and two from the DIB population) expressed discomfort with all the potential applications of AI but comfort with blocking foreign militaries from deploying AI (indicating discomfort with AI). These findings support that while these extreme viewpoints may attract attention, they are atypical of these populations overall.

---

[1] Rory Cellan-Jones, "Stephen Hawking—Will AI Kill or Save Mankind?" *BBC News*, October 20, 2016.

Trust in Institutions and Individuals

The second section of the survey inquired about the degree of trust that respondents feel for a variety of institutions in U.S. society. These institutions included the U.S. government, DoD, and U.S. technology companies, along with several other societal institutions included to provide a baseline against which to compare.[2] Additionally, respondents were asked to describe their level of trust in various groups of individuals associated with those institutions. For example, respondents were asked their opinion about both the U.S. military and uniformed military officers working at DoD. The results are presented in Figures 4.4 through 4.10.

For this analysis, the research team combined individuals who responded that they had "a great deal" with those expressing "quite a lot" of trust and denoted them as having a "high" degree of trust in the listed institution or member of an institution. Individuals who answered "very little" or "none" were considered to have a "low" degree of trust in the listed institution or member of an institution. Individuals who answered "some" were not included in either the "high" or "low" trust grouping for that institution.

Trust for Institutions

Trust levels in the listed institutions varied greatly across the three respondent populations and across the different types of institutions.

First, relatively few of the survey respondents expressed a high degree of trust in the U.S. federal government, with a plurality of each population having only "some" trust in that institution.

In contrast, the DIB population trusted the U.S. military and U.S. intelligence agencies significantly more than did the other two populations. Only 26 percent of the Silicon Valley Employees population and 32 percent

FIGURE 4.4
Respondents' Trust in Governmental Institutions

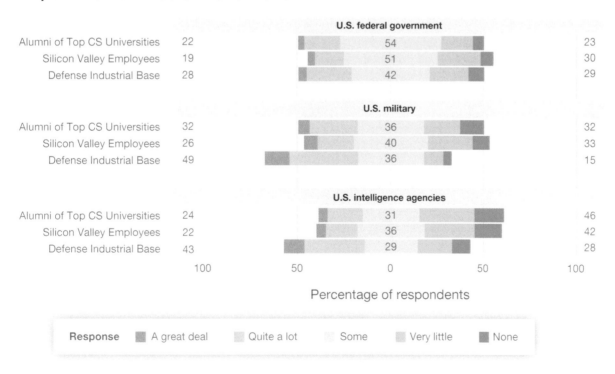

---

[2] These baseline institutions and individuals were taken from either Gallup, undated-a, or Rainie, Keeter, and Perrin, 2019.

FIGURE 4.5

Respondents' Trust in Technology Companies

U.S. technology companies, such as the FAANGM

Alumni of Top CS Universities	16	35 49
Silicon Valley Employees	28	46 27
Defense Industrial Base	14	37 49

Employer

Alumni of Top CS Universities	59	31 10
Silicon Valley Employees	56	34 10
Defense Industrial Base	56	32 12

100   50   0   50   100

Percentage of respondents

Response   ■ A great deal   ■ Quite a lot   Some   ■ Very little   ■ None

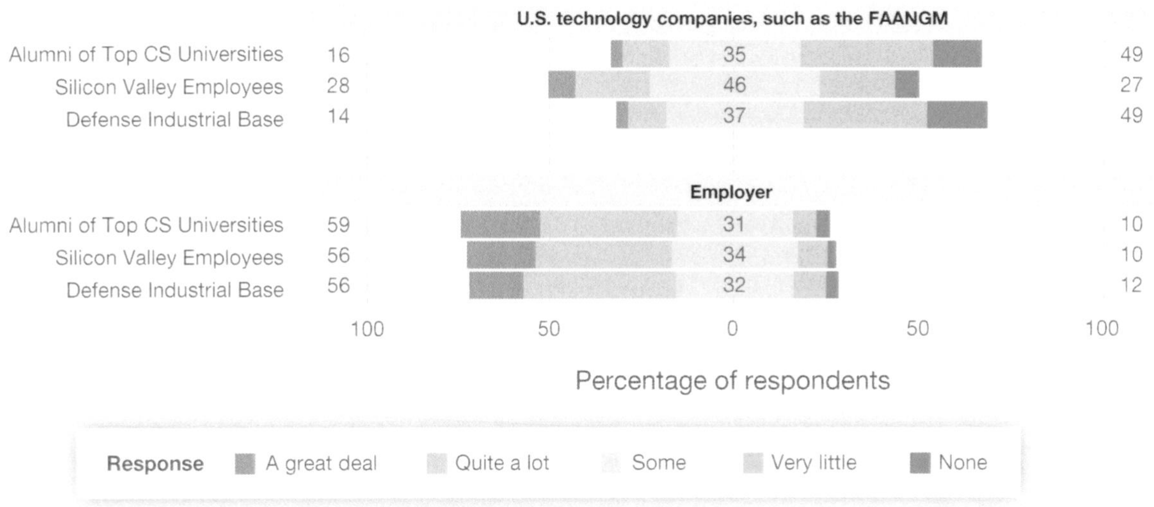

NOTE: FAANGM = Facebook, Apple, Amazon, Netflix, Google, and Microsoft.

of the Alumni of Top CS Universities population had a high degree of trust in the military. In comparison, in Gallup's annual poll, about 70 percent of the general public reports a high degree of trust in the military.[3]

Each of the populations expressed greater trust in their own employer than in any other institution listed in the survey.

The populations varied more greatly in the degree of trust they placed in U.S. technology companies, such as Facebook, Apple, Amazon, Netflix, Google, or Microsoft. Both the DIB and Alumni of Top CS Universities survey populations expressed less trust in these companies than in any other listed option. However, the Silicon Valley Employees population trusted these companies more than did the Alumni of Top CS Universities and the DIB; even so, less than one-third of the Silicon Valley Employees respondents expressed a high degree of trust in these companies. Interestingly, members of the Silicon Valley Employees population expressed significantly lower levels of trust in U.S. technology companies than they did in their own employer, even though all of the respondents from that population worked for one of the listed companies. This finding suggests workers have a lower degree of trust in technology companies that they do not work for than they do in the company that they interact with every day.

Finally, on average, each of the survey populations had a relatively high degree of trust in U.S. colleges and universities and a relatively low degree of trust in the media (Figure 4.6). Results from this survey for the media and the medical system were similar to those of Gallup's polling results from the U.S. general public, with 21 percent of Gallup respondents expressing a great deal or quite a lot of confidence in newspapers, 16 percent saying the same about television news, and 44 percent having a high degree of trust in the medical system.[4]

The research team used a regression model to evaluate the "trust in institutions" findings to test whether the differences in population outcomes were because of the population and not because of correlated variables. For a little over one-third of the institutions in question (38 percent), being a member of the Alumni of Top CS Universities or Silicon Valley Employees populations was statistically significantly associated with

---

[3] Gallup phrased their trust question slightly differently than did this survey. Gallup asks how much confidence the respondent has in the institution, while this survey asked whether the respondent trusted the institution to act in a way that the respondent agreed with (see Gallup, undated-a).

[4] Gallup does not ask about U.S. colleges and universities (see Gallup, undated-a).

FIGURE 4.6
Respondents' Trust in Other Societal Institutions

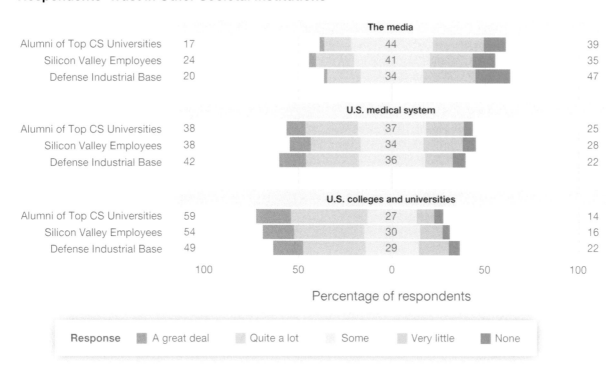

The media

Alumni of Top CS Universities	17	44	39
Silicon Valley Employees	24	41	35
Defense Industrial Base	20	34	47

U.S. medical system

Alumni of Top CS Universities	38	37	25
Silicon Valley Employees	38	34	28
Defense Industrial Base	42	36	22

U.S. colleges and universities

Alumni of Top CS Universities	59	27	14
Silicon Valley Employees	54	30	16
Defense Industrial Base	49	29	22

100   50   0   50   100

Percentage of respondents

Response   ■ A great deal   ■ Quite a lot   ■ Some   ■ Very little   ■ None

trust. For half the questions, age was a statistically significant factor, and, for 38 percent, gender was a significant factor, suggesting that demographic factors also help explain attitudes. When gender was a significant predictor, it indicated that women had less trust in institutions than did men, and, when age was significant, it indicated that older respondents had more trust. These results are consistent with results from surveys of the U.S. public that have found that age often correlates positively with trust in societal institutions.[5] However, membership in the various survey populations remained a significant factor, even after the complicating factor of age was considered. None of the other variables made statistically significant contributions.

Trust in Members of Institutions

As shown in Figures 4.7 through 4.10, trust levels in individual members of the listed institutions displayed some interesting patterns compared with the trust levels in the institutions themselves. First, all three populations ranked individuals in leadership positions—U.S. elected officials, political appointees leading U.S. federal agencies, and corporate chief executive officers (CEOs) of U.S. technology companies—the lowest in terms of their overall trust. In contrast, other types of employees working in the same institution—whether they were civil servants, military officers, or software engineers—had a high-trust score at least 30 percentage points higher than did their leadership. These results are reinforced by the *adhocracy* culture that predominates among software engineers and other technical staff, which rejects rules and hierarchy in favor of autonomy and individual initiative for rank-and-file engineers.[6]

---

[5]   John Gramlich, "Young Americans Are Less Trusting of Other People—and Key Institutions—Than Their Elders," Pew Research Center, August 6, 2019.

[6]   Donald Sull, Charles Sull, and Andrew Chamberlain, *Measuring Culture in Leading Companies*, Cambridge, Mass.: MIT Sloan Management Review, 2019; and Amir Grinstein and Arieh Goldman, "Characterizing the Technology Firm: An Exploratory Study," *Research Policy*, Vol. 35, 2006.

FIGURE 4.7

Respondents' Trust in Institutional Leaders

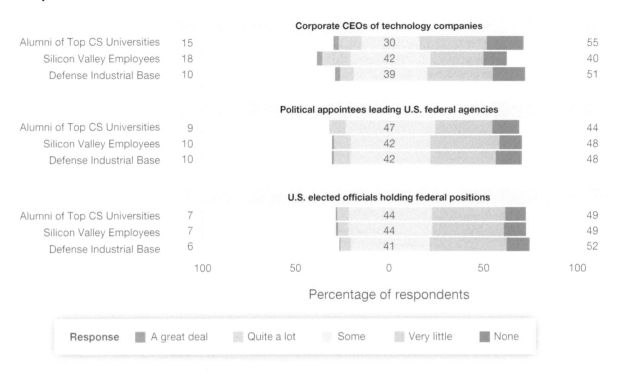

FIGURE 4.8

Respondents' Trust in Software Engineers

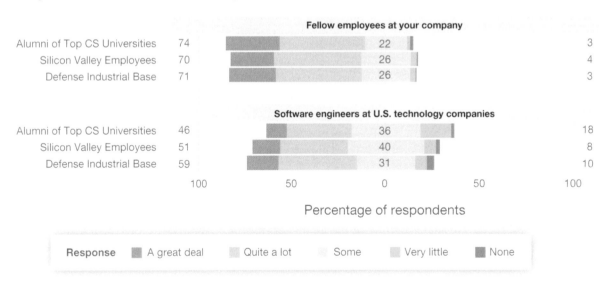

Additionally, all three populations agreed on the individuals whom they trusted the most. Doctors and other medical professionals received the highest trust ranking from each group of respondents, followed by fellow employees. Professors at U.S. universities and colleges were also highly trusted by each of the survey populations, although members of the DIB population trusted them slightly less than did the other two populations. The high regard for medical professionals, especially during the COVID-19 global pandemic, is not surprising. Similarly, the high regard for one's own coworkers matches the greater degree of trust for one's

FIGURE 4.9

Respondents' Trust in Members of Other Societal Institutions

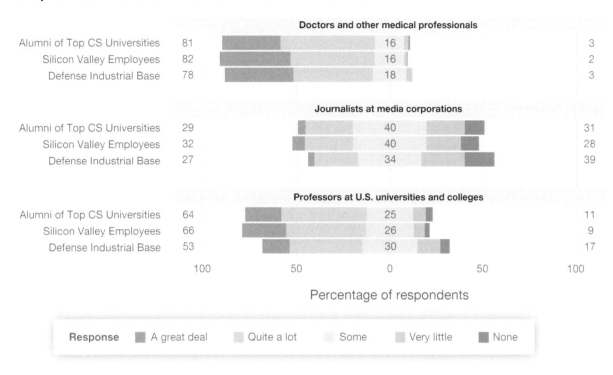

FIGURE 4.10

Respondents' Trust in Government Employees and Military Personnel

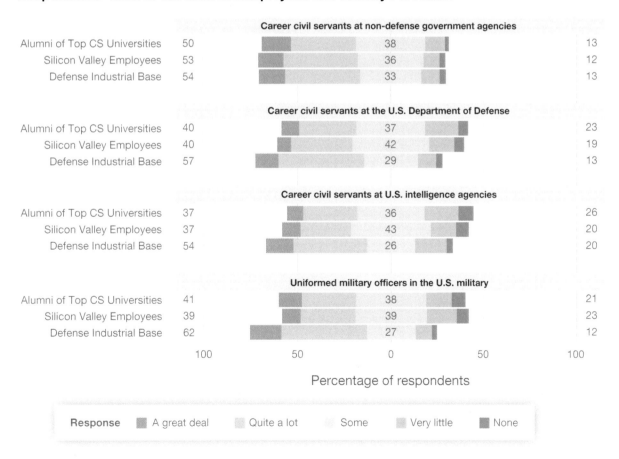

own company. Survey respondents seemed to express a higher degree of trust across the board for individuals and institutions with whom they frequently interact and whom they feel that they understand.[7]

All three populations reported similar levels of trust for software engineers working at U.S. technology companies and for the two categories of individuals working for DoD: uniformed military officers and career civil servants. The Silicon Valley Employees population showed the greatest degree of divergence, with at least a 10-percentage-point gap between the number of individuals reporting a high degree of trust in software engineers and those reporting trust in DoD employees (regardless of whether they are military officers or civil servants).

Additionally, Figure 4.10 shows that both the Silicon Valley Employees population and the Alumni of Top CS Universities population reported at least a 10-percentage-point gain in trust for career civil servants working for nondefense government agencies compared with career civil servants working at DoD. In contrast, software engineers in the DIB expressed a similar level of trust for military officers and civil servants working at DoD as they did for career civil servants working for nondefense government agencies.

The research team also evaluated trust in groups and people within institutions to test whether or not the differences were significantly associated with population membership. For slightly fewer than half of the institutions in question (42 percent), being a member of the Alumni of Top CS Universities or Silicon Valley Employees populations was a statistically significant predictor of trust. For half the questions, age and gender were statistically significant predictors. Other variables were rarely significant. As with institutions, when gender was a significant predictor, it indicated that women had less trust in groups than did men, and when age was significant, it indicated that younger respondents had less trust.

Perception of Global Threats

The third section of the survey examined the survey participants' perception of a variety of potential threats to the United States. First, the respondents were asked to provide their perception of eight types of global threat, some of which might require a military response. The results are listed in Figure 4.11.

All three populations agreed that cyberattacks represent the greatest degree of threat among the options presented. At least 66 percent of respondents in each surveyed population ranked cyberattacks as a critical threat to the United States, and more than 90 percent of each population rated this as either a critical threat or an important threat. Two of the populations—Silicon Valley Employees and Alumni of Top CS Universities—considered global climate change to have a similar level of threat to cyberattacks, with slightly more respondents categorizing global climate change as a critical threat but slightly fewer categorizing it as either a critical or an important threat. DIB software engineers viewed global climate change as a less significant threat than did the other survey populations, with about 15 percentage points fewer DIB respondents viewing it as a critical threat. The Silicon Valley Employees and Alumni of Top CS Universities populations saw all types of military threats (whether conventional, intra-state, terrorist, or nuclear) as a somewhat lower threat than cyberattacks and global climate change. Still, approximately half of each population saw these threats as either a critical or important threat to the United States. And compared with the Silicon Valley Employees and Alumni of Top CS Universities populations, DIB engineers rated every listed threat option except for global climate change as more concerning. The degree of difference between the DIB engineers and the other populations was the smallest over armed conflicts within nations and nuclear weapon attacks.

---

[7] Studies in organizational trust have also found that familiarity with an organization increases trust in it. For one example, see Ranjay Gulati and Maxim Sytch, "Does Familiarity Breed Trust? Revisiting the Antecedents of Trust," *Managerial and Decision Economics*, Vol. 29, Nos. 2–3, 2008.

FIGURE 4.11

Percentage of Respondents Who Consider a Threat to Be Critical

Would you say that the following represent a very serious threat to the United States, a moderately serious threat, just a slight threat, or no threat at all?

Percentage of respondents

| Response | Very serious threat | Moderately serious threat | Slight threat | No threat |

Comparing these results with surveys of the general public reveals some notable similarities and differences. Poll results from Gallup and the Chicago Council on Global Affairs showed overall agreement with the survey respondents that cyber threats pose the greatest danger to the United States.[8] However, RAND's survey respondents for this study perceived a much lower degree of threat from international terrorism compared with the U.S public as a whole. Approximately 70 percent of respondents from surveys of the general public considered international terrorism to be a critical threat to the United States; in contrast, fewer than 33 percent of DIB software engineers and 20 percent of Silicon Valley Employees or Alumni of Top CS Universities respondents agreed.

Additionally, the research team asked respondents to describe the degree of threat they perceive from four countries that DoD considers to be strategic competitors: China, Iran, North Korea, and Russia. Figure 4.12 displays these results.

All three surveyed populations perceive China and Russia to be the greatest potential threats to the United States, with nearly 80 percent of respondents considering each to be either a very serious or a moderately

FIGURE 4.12
Significance of Threat from Strategic Competitors

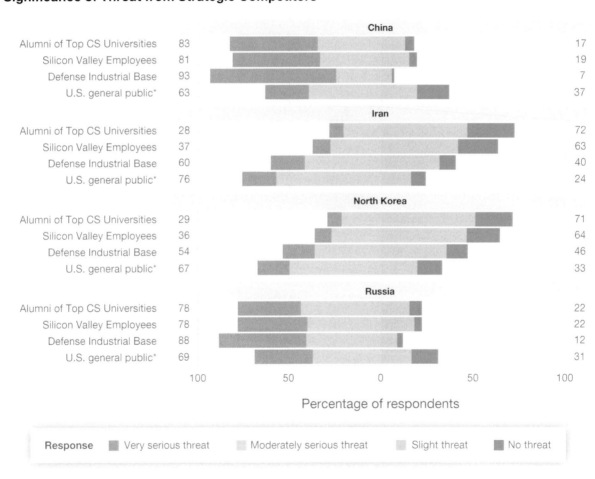

SOURCE: Authors' analysis of SSRS, 2020.
NOTE: *Survey data for the U.S. general public is from SSRS polling for CNN conducted January 16–19, 2020.

---

[8] Megan Brenan, "Cyberterrorism Tops List of 11 Potential Threats to the United States," Gallup, March 22, 2021; Smeltz et al., 2019.

serious threat to the United States. A plurality of respondents in the Silicon Valley Employees and Alumni of Top CS Universities populations viewed Iran and North Korea as only slight threats to the United States; DIB engineers were split between viewing these countries as a moderately serious threat and a slight threat. In all cases, the DIB population perceived a greater degree of threat from each potential adversary than did the Silicon Valley Employees and Alumni of Top CS Universities populations. This pattern of responses also differs from that of the U.S. public, which sees less of a difference in the degree of threat that each of these four countries poses to the United States.

This section of the survey—on perceived threat—showed the most consistent association of population membership with attitudes when the data were analyzed using the regression model. For 10 of the 11 questions, being in either the Alumni of Top CS Universities or the Silicon Valley Employees population was a statistically significant factor in predicting responses regarding threat perceptions.

Age was a significant predictor in just over half the questions, and gender was a predictor in just over a third. This finding confirms that most DIB respondents perceive global threats to be of greater concern than do the other two populations; however, the overall magnitude of the difference is only modest.

Justifications for the Use of Military Force

The fourth section of the survey queried respondents' opinions about what types of global crises might justify the use of military force by the United States. The scenarios ranged from retaliating for attacks that had killed U.S. civilians or service members, to responding to requests from allies for assistance, to preempting an expected attack on U.S. military personnel. Figure 4.13 displays the survey results.

Each of the survey populations expressed the strong belief that military force was justified when responding to attacks that had killed U.S. civilians or service members. Interestingly, defending North Atlantic Treaty Organization (NATO) allies received a similar level of support, with nearly 90 percent of respondents in each of the three populations finding this use of force to be justified. Wars to uphold international agreements, such as a treaty or U.N. resolution, were also strongly supported with at least 66 percent of each survey population finding these kinds of wars to be justified.

In contrast, responding to a non-NATO ally's request for assistance against foreign aggression drew a lower level of support (compared with similar requests from a NATO ally). It is unclear how much the two specific example nations listed in the question—Saudi Arabia and the Philippines—might have affected the responses (the full question is shown in question 11 of Section G of the survey in Appendix B). In particular, a 2019 survey conducted by the Chicago Council on Global Affairs found that 78 percent of respondents expressed the belief that the U.S. relationship with Japan strengthened its national security, while 60 percent of respondents believed the same about its relationship with the Philippines, and only 45 percent of respondents felt that the U.S. relationship with Saudi Arabia improved U.S. national security.[9] Consequently, specifying non-NATO allies that have received a strong level of support from the U.S. public—such as Japan or South Korea—might have resulted in a greater percentage of respondents considering military action to protect those allies to be justified. Regardless, the data indicate that responding to a request for assistance from some U.S. allies will be less supported by the surveyed populations than would a request to defend a NATO ally.

Finally, wars over unpopulated territory or to break an economic embargo received the lowest levels of support among all the hypothetical scenarios listed, as Figure 4.14 illustrates. Across all the surveyed popula-

---

[9]   Smeltz et al., 2019.

FIGURE 4.13

Defending the United States and Its Allies

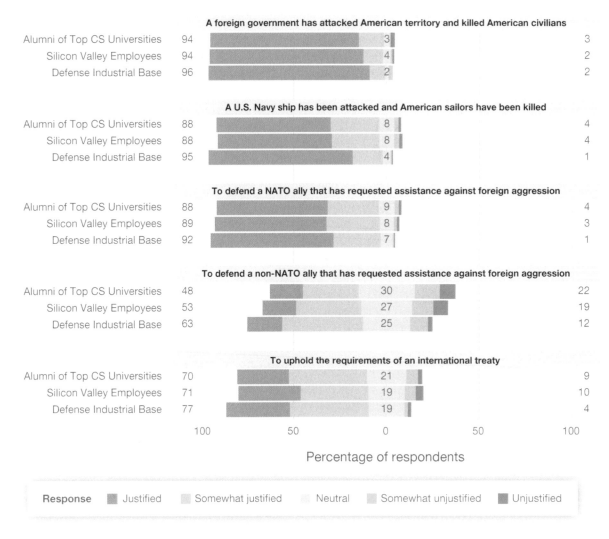

tions, no more than 35 percent of respondents considered the use of military force to be justified under these circumstances.

Overall, respondents found the hypothetical use of military force to be justified far more often than they found it to be unjustified among the hypothetical scenarios that the survey presented. For only two of these scenarios did more respondents consider the use of military force to be unjustified than did the number of respondents who believed it would be justified. Also, similar percentages of respondents across the three surveyed populations found the use of military force to be justified with most of the scenarios.

One final scenario with a notable variance in support described a hypothetical strike to preempt an expected attack on U.S. service members. The DIB survey population was more likely to find such a conflict justified than were the other two survey populations (Figure 4.15).

Regression analysis of response patterns to the force justification questions showed that population had a statistically significant association with responses for Alumni of Top CS Universities in more than half (7 of 12). This figure was just under half (5 of 12) for Silicon Valley Employees. However, for these questions, population was much more likely to be the only factor that was statistically significant. Age was significant in only two cases, and gender in five cases, while the other variables showed negligible association.

Figure 4.14
Responding to Foreign Crises

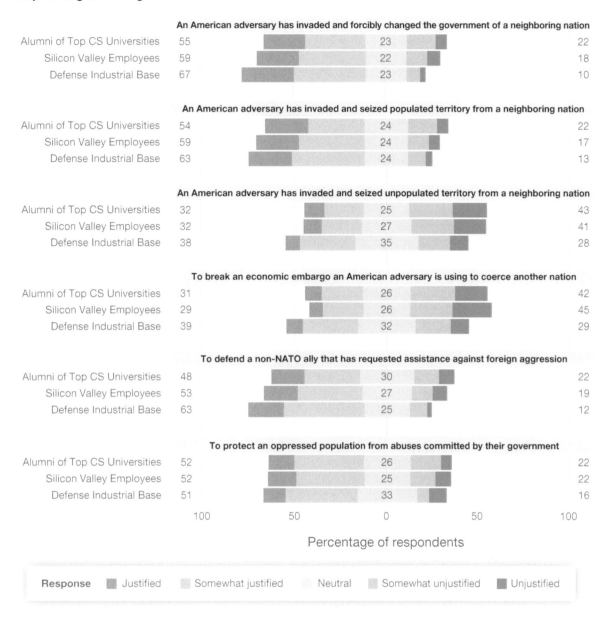

Information Sources and Other Influences

The research team combined the results of several open-ended questions, questions from across the survey, and demographic information to understand factors that might be associated with particular trends in responses.

News Sources

The survey sought to identify the sources that respondents said that they turn to for news about current events, world affairs, and science and technology developments. As shown in Figure 4.16, the source that survey participants most frequently cited as one of their top two for news was the *New York Times*, followed

FIGURE 4.15
Preemptive Strikes

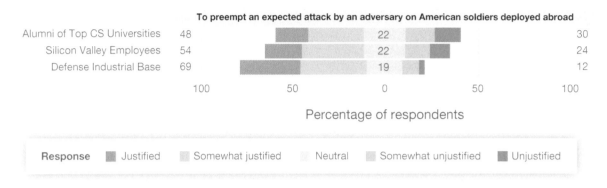

To preempt an expected attack by an adversary on American soldiers deployed abroad

Alumni of Top CS Universities	48	22	30
Silicon Valley Employees	54	22	24
Defense Industrial Base	69	19	12

Percentage of respondents

Response ■ Justified ■ Somewhat justified ■ Neutral ■ Somewhat unjustified ■ Unjustified

FIGURE 4.16
Most Commonly Identified News Sources (All Survey Populations)

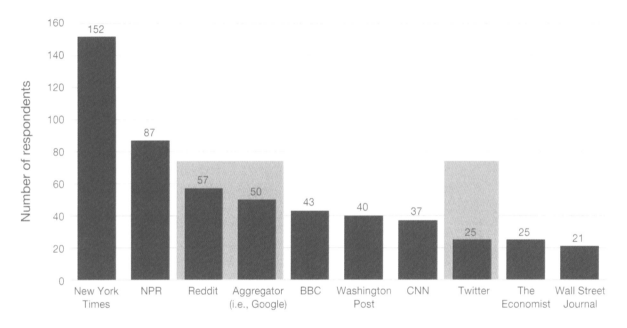

NOTES: Shading denotes aggregated news sources, those providing user-curated content. Respondents did not specify how they accessed a given news source (e.g., print or digital).

by National Public Radio (NPR). These sources may be considered general media (i.e., focusing on such areas as policy, culture, technology, and health). In contrast, Reddit and Twitter, the third and eighth most-popular sources, are curated by participants and, therefore, could be interpreted as a channel with crowd-sourced views. Respondents typically did not identify specific subreddit threads they follow, but these might include forums specific to AI, DoD news, technology trends, or other topics. News aggregators (e.g., Google), the fourth most-popular option, could work in a similar way because algorithms curate them based on user preferences.

In addition to these top ten commonly identified news sources, other, less commonly identified news sources (either as potential influences or indirect social media sources) include some talk shows (e.g., those often referred to by their hosts, such as Steven Colbert, Trevor Noah, John Oliver), podcasts (e.g., with host Ben Shapiro), non–U.S.-based sources (e.g., echo.msk.ru, Le Monde Diplomatique), Breitbart, Hacker News,

Ars Technica, The Intercept, Apple News, and various other social media platforms. Although respondents typically did not specify the channel for their particular source (e.g., print or digital), broadcast television was not predominant among the news sources mentioned.

The type of news that each population regularly consumes showed some variation. As shown in Figure 4.17, although the *New York Times* was the most commonly identified news source across all respondents, respondents from the Silicon Valley Employees population were more than twice as likely as DIB respondents to select the *New York Times* as their preferred regular news source. In contrast, NPR was one of the most commonly identified news sources across all respondents, but more respondents from the DIB population (15.2 percent) identified NPR as their regular news source than did any other population group.

Finally, the data demonstrate that these populations rely primarily on digital sources for their news. More than 50 percent of respondents indicated that they read websites of media organizations every day to get their news. The next most popular option, social media sites, was used daily by only 20 percent of respondents to consume news. In comparison, these populations were substantially less likely to rely on television as their primary source of news, with only 8 percent of respondents indicating that they consume news from this source every day. In contrast, the latest Gallup polls of the U.S. population show that about 33 percent of Americans still watch daily televised news broadcasts.[10] Figure 4.18 details survey respondents' use of various news sources.

Key Events Anchoring Perceptions

The survey inquired about events and issues that had shaped respondents' views about DoD's potential use of AI (see Figure 4.19). Overwhelmingly, drones were the most frequently mentioned issue, with 24 percent of

FIGURE 4.17

Respondents Receive News from Similar Sources, Regardless of Employer

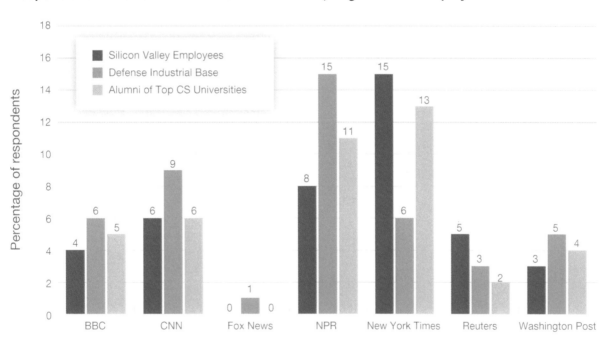

NOTE: Categories are not mutually exclusive. Respondents could indicate multiple news sources.

___

10 Gallup, undated-b.

FIGURE 4.18

How Often Survey Participants Get Their News from Various Sources

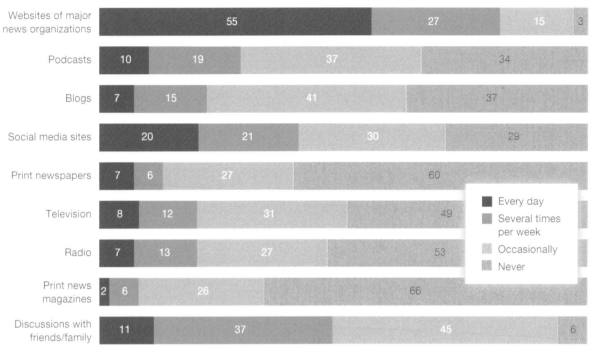

FIGURE 4.19

Key Events and Issues Influencing Understanding of Department of Defense Use of Artificial Intelligence

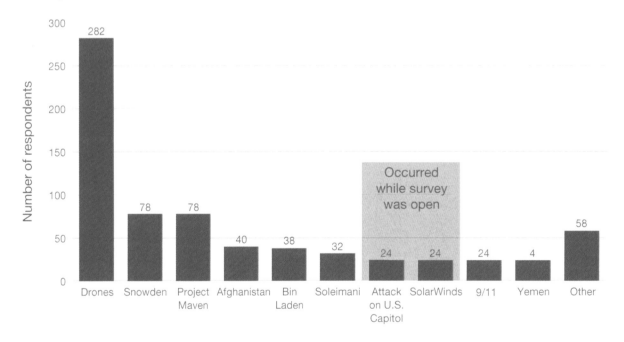

NOTE: The attack on the U.S. Capitol occurred on January 6, 2021, and media reports about the SolarWinds hack began in December 2020. Both events occurred during the period when the survey was open, from December 2020 through April 2021. Respondents were asked to list one or two events that had shaped their understanding of DoD use of AI.

all respondents referencing the use of drones (across multiple events) as anchoring their views of DoD's use of AI. Example references of events include "drone strikes at weddings" (Silicon Valley Employees respondent), a "vague sense of numerous deaths by U.S. drones in foreign countries " (DIB), and uses of AI "to help controlling drone flotillas, and defend against them" (DIB). Looking across the three populations, DIB employees were significantly less likely to reference drones than were Alumni of Top CS Universities (at the alpha = 0.01 level).

In addition to drone strikes, other events and issues ranged from prominent individuals killed by the U.S. military, foreign countries where the U.S. military operates, cybersecurity breaches, and notable domestic events. Because respondents were able to enter free text, some redundancy in responses and overlaps in response categories occurred. For example, a respondent might be alluding to Kunduz Hospital in Afghanistan or drone strikes in Afghanistan/Yemen. In these cases, the responses were counted in multiple categories. Other issues and events that were identified, albeit less frequently than the ones included in the figure, include a reference to any election (n = 21), the Patriot Act (n = 19), and the Joint Enterprise Defense Infrastructure contract (n = 14).

Familiarity with the Military

Survey participants were also asked several questions about their personal ties to the military. First, respondents were asked whether they had previously served in the military—either in the U.S. military or the military of another country. The data show that relatively few respondents in these populations had previously served (see Figure 4.20). Only eight respondents (~1 percent) from the Silicon Valley Employees population and only 11 respondents (~5 percent) from the Alumni of Top CS Universities population had previously served in the U.S. military, as compared with 38 respondents (~21 percent) from the DIB population. In contrast, 22 respondents (~3 percent) from the Silicon Valley Employees population, four respondents (~2 percent) from the Alumni of Top CS Universities population, and one (less than 1 percent) from the DIB had previously served in a foreign military.

FIGURE 4.20
Survey Respondents with Prior Military Service

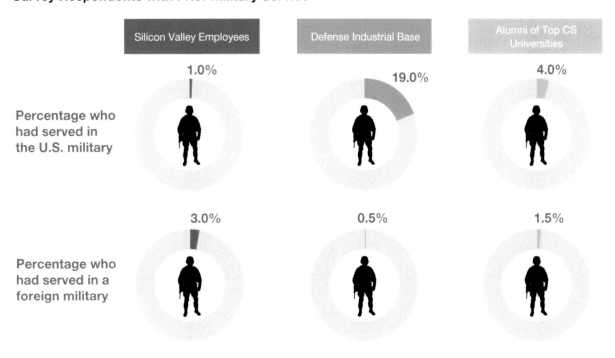

Additionally, participants were asked whether various family members or other individuals close to them had served or were serving in the military of any country. The results are shown in Figure 4.21. As the data show, DIB software engineers are the most likely to have a close friend or family member serving in the military. Only 25 percent of this group was not close to anyone with prior military experience. In contrast, individuals in the Silicon Valley Employees population were the least likely to know anyone with military experience. More than half of the respondents in this population had no close friends or family with prior military experience.

Correlations Across Sections

In addition to analyzing the sections of the survey individually, the research team also analyzed the data to determine whether any patterns emerged among responses to survey questions across individual sections of the survey. The strongest such association was between the level of trust that an individual felt in the U.S. military, comfort with the potential military uses for AI, and the degree of threat the respondent perceived from global threats. Survey respondents from the Silicon Valley Employees population were split between those who had a high level of trust in the military—characterized as individuals who said they had "a great deal" or "quite a lot" of trust in the U.S. military—and those who expressed a low level of trust in the military—characterized as individuals who responded with "very little" or "none" when asked how much trust they had that the military would act in a way that they would agree with. Dividing the respondents along those lines, the research team then compared their responses to the other questions against each other.

FIGURE 4.21
Survey Respondents Who Have Family or Friends with Prior Military Service

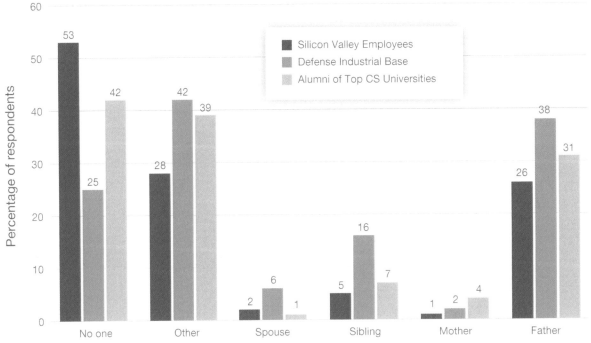

NOTE: Respondents could select more than one category. Totals do not add to 100 percent because the categories are not mutually exclusive.

FIGURE 4.22

Split Between Silicon Valley Employees Respondents with High Trust and Low Trust in the U.S. Military

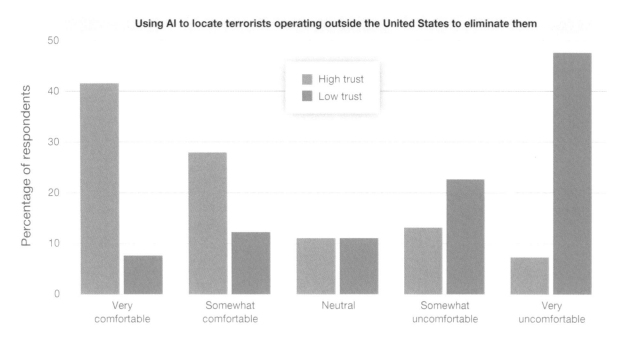

Figure 4.22 shows one particularly notable result when the survey data for one hypothetical scenario involving the use of AI by DoD—using AI to locate terrorists—are compared across the two groups.

In results not shown here, all of the scenarios involving the potential use of lethal force by AI, regardless of whether the AI was supervised or unsupervised, had a meaningful divergence between individuals in the high-trust group and those in the low-trust group. Additionally, questions concerning survey respondents' perceptions of global threats with a military dimension—such as international terrorist attacks or rising military capabilities in potentially hostile foreign countries—showed a similar split, where respondents with a high level of trust in the military perceived these options to be a greater threat and respondents with a lower level of trust in the military perceived them to be a lesser threat.

Some other response options in the survey questions on trust in institutions demonstrated a similar association. For example, splitting respondents by their degree of trust in U.S. intelligence agencies, such as the Central Intelligence Agency (CIA) or National Security Agency (NSA), resulted in a similar pattern in the data. However, the pattern was clearest for the split on attitudes of trust regarding the U.S. military.

This analysis cannot determine the causal relationships among these observations. Different levels of trust in the military could shape the perception of global threats, different perceptions of the degree of threat from global problems could shape the trust level that respondents have in the U.S. military, or a different, unmeasured factor could be shaping both the level of trust respondents have in the military and the degree of threat that they perceive from global military threats.

Of note, the most pronounced similarity among responses to groups of survey items involving the degree of trust in members of institutions was the degree of trust that respondents felt in career civil servants working at other non-defense U.S. government agencies and the degree of threat respondents perceived from global climate change. Respondents with a high degree of trust in this group perceived climate change as a significantly greater threat than did respondents with a low degree of trust.

Summary of Regression Results

The regression analysis found that survey population was the most common variable associated with survey responses. For 64 percent of the questions, the Alumni of Top CS Universities population's responses had a statistically significant difference from those of the DIB population at the $p = 0.05$ level. The difference was statistically significant in 44 percent of questions at the $p = 0.01$ level. This was the most frequently significant variable, followed by the Silicon Valley Employees population, which was significantly different from the DIB population for 51 percent of questions at the $p = 0.05$ level and 31 percent at the $p = 0.01$ level. The next most common variables to show significant associations with responses were gender and age, which were both frequently significant (both were significant for 44 percent of questions at the $p = 0.05$ level and 25 percent and 19 percent, respectively, at the $p = 0.01$ level). None of the remaining variables was significant at the $p = 0.05$ level in more than ten questions.

These findings indicate that, although other factors (specifically, gender and age) are associated with attitudes about comfort with AI, trust, threat perception, and force justification, the most frequent predictor among survey respondents was population (i.e., employer affiliation).

This finding was most pronounced in two question categories: comfort around lethal use of AI and perceptions of threats. For all but two of the 18 questions in these sections, the regressions found that population was a statistically significant predictor at the $p = 0.05$ level. In only three instances was affiliation with the Alumni of Top CS Universities population not significant, and in only six instances was Silicon Valley Employees affiliation not significant at the $p = 0.01$ level. Though population variables were significant for roughly half the questions overall, these two areas were the most consistent.

To visualize these findings, the research team used box plots to plot the significance of all the variables for all questions, sorted by question category (see Figure 4.23). The order of the variables reflects the median significance of that variable in being associated with differences in responses, across all questions. Lines indicating key significance thresholds (1.96 for the alpha = 0.05 level, 2.58 for the alpha = 0.01 level) were added. The output shows that the four variables on the left (years of experience, military connection, residency in California or Washington, residency in New York or New Jersey) were rarely significant. The next most frequent variables were age and gender. Membership in the Silicon Valley Employees or Alumni of Top CS Universities survey populations were the most likely to be significant with respect to association with different responses, in many cases at the higher threshold. This was especially true for the key question categories of comfort with AI and perception of global threats.

FIGURE 4.23

Distribution of Statistical Significance, by Variable and Survey Category

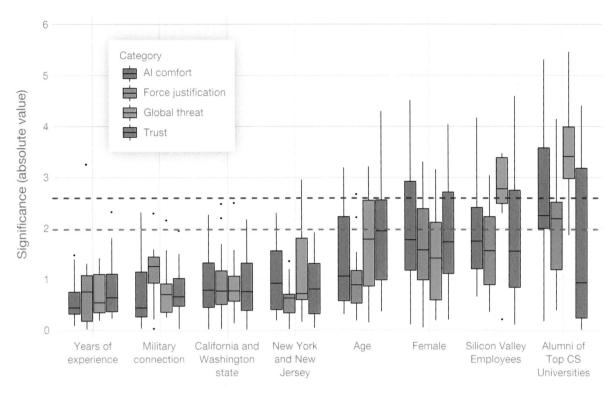

CHAPTER FIVE

Key Findings and Conclusions

This chapter provides the overarching conclusions and summarizes the key findings of the survey that support each of those conclusions.

There Does Not Appear to Be an Unbridgeable Divide Between Silicon Valley and the Department of Defense

The survey data show that respondents from the Silicon Valley Employees and Alumni of Top CS Universities populations are comfortable with a wide variety of military applications for AI. Large majorities of respondents expressed their comfort with using AI to support battlefield operations or to protect U.S. service members in ways that do not require the use of lethal force. Most survey respondents also expressed their comfort with AI recommending actions that involve the use of lethal force if the final decision remains under human control. As a group, private sector technology workers who are not employed within the DIB perceive global threats similarly to their counterparts at defense contractors, and they believe that using military force is justified to respond to many kinds of aggressive behavior from U.S. adversaries or to protect U.S. allies. All in all, these results illustrate that most of the United States' AI experts do not oppose the basic mission of DoD or the use of AI for many military applications.

There Is a Meaningful Difference in the Comfort Level for Artificial Intelligence Applications That Involve the Use of Lethal Force

Although a majority of survey respondents were comfortable with scenarios in which AI would recommend the use of lethal force, about one-third of respondents from the three surveyed Silicon Valley technology corporations were uncomfortable with these use cases for AI. In contrast, less than one-fifth of software engineers in the DIB who responded to the survey expressed similar opinions. In particular, AI applications directed at identifying terrorists split the Silicon Valley Employees and Alumni of Top CS Universities populations nearly evenly, with a plurality of respondents expressing discomfort with using AI for this purpose.

Tech Workers Have Low Levels of Trust in Leaders—Even Their Own

The survey data demonstrate that software engineers and other technology workers have low levels of trust in individuals who hold leadership positions. This is true regardless of the type of organization involved—technology workers trust CEOs of technology companies almost as little as they trust elected officials or the heads of federal agencies. This difference is reinforced by the vastly different workplace culture to which many technology workers are accustomed. Unlike military organizations, software companies are typically run as *adhocracies*. In this type of organizational culture, members emphasize autonomy and typically show a disdain toward rules and hierarchy. Consequently, simply winning over the leadership of these companies will not cause engineers to fall into line behind them automatically; instead, a broader and more deliberate outreach effort would be more likely to help DoD earn these individuals' trust.

Tech Workers Are Most Concerned About Cyber Threats

Perhaps unsurprisingly, the survey data demonstrate that respondents overwhelmingly viewed cyber threats as a critical threat to the United States. Other types of military and national security threats were seen as relatively less important, with only about one-fifth of respondents from the private sector viewing them as a critical threat. Technical employees at defense contractors agreed with this assessment that cyber threats represent a substantially greater danger to the United States than do other military threats. Silicon Valley Employees respondents also agreed that China and Russia presented a meaningful danger to the United States, with about four-fifths of respondents viewing those countries as a critical or an important threat. At the same time, survey participants were less convinced of the potential threat from Iran and North Korea, with a plurality viewing those nations as only a moderate threat to the United States.

Tech Workers Support the Use of Military Force to Defend Against Foreign Aggression

Survey respondents strongly supported using military force to defend the United States and its NATO allies from foreign aggression, with nearly 90 percent of participants finding the use of military force to be justified under these circumstances. A majority of respondents also expressed the belief that the use of military force would be justified to defend foreign nations from attacks by U.S. adversaries in a variety of scenarios. Although a greater percentage of DIB engineers found the use of military force to be justified compared with their counterparts from the nonmilitary commercial sector (Silicon Valley Employees and Alumni of Top CS Universities), the degree of difference was relatively small, and these populations tended to agree more than they disagreed.

However, support across all types of respondents dropped significantly when survey participants were asked their opinion of defending non-NATO allies, such as Saudi Arabia or the Philippines, compared with defending NATO allies under the same circumstances. Potential military conflicts over small islands or other unpopulated territory also drew weaker support, with only one-third of respondents considering the use of military force to be justified under these circumstances. These results could indicate a lower degree of support for the use of military force in response to certain types of crises in the Middle East or East Asia.

Silicon Valley Tech Workers Have Little Personal Connection to the Military

Employees of Silicon Valley technology firms reported a lower degree of familiarity with—and personal ties to—DoD compared with software engineers employed by defense contractors. At the largest Silicon Valley software companies, almost three times as many individuals had served in a foreign military as had served in the U.S. military. Similarly, more than half of the participants from Silicon Valley technology companies reported that they did not know anyone close to them who had ever served in the military. In contrast, one-fifth of DIB software engineers had previously served in the U.S. military, and only one-quarter of DIB employees did not know anyone close to them who either was serving or had previously served.

CHAPTER SIX

Future Opportunities and Areas for Further Investigation

The survey provided insights into attitudes and views concerning potential military uses of AI among leading technology and AI developers. Understanding the full implications—and impact—of these findings for DoD would require additional research, as would developing potential strategies to mitigate poor perceptions and capitalize on positive ones. The survey was designed to understand similarities and differences in attitudes among and between populations, and thus should not be used to extrapolate benefits, costs, or risks of current or any alternative DoD strategy or policy.

Nonetheless, the results of the survey suggest potential areas to explore for strengthening DoD's relationship with experts and leading high-tech companies that are not traditionally part of the DIB. Using the survey's findings and the team's conclusions, this chapter identifies areas for further exploration that may strengthen the relationship between DoD and leading high-tech companies.

Topics of Shared Interest

The survey results indicate that there is general agreement among respondents that cyber threats are among the most significant national security threats facing the United States. As nation states and criminal organizations continue to increase their proficiency with cyber operations and develop more advanced cyber capabilities, their effects will permeate U.S. daily life more deeply. The Office of the Director of National Intelligence 2021 Annual Threat Assessment includes cyber among its list of the most serious threats to the United States.[1] In addition, the White House Interim National Security Strategic Guidance states that cybersecurity is a top priority.[2] Exploring more applications at the intersection of AI and cybersecurity may present opportunities for enhancing the relationship between DoD and the leading AI technology companies.

Expanding Engagements

The survey results indicate that respondents place more trust in their co-workers than they do in corporate leadership or other individuals in senior leadership positions. An area for further exploration is whether expanding engagements between personnel involved with military operations and DoD technical experts directly with software engineers and individual contributors (nonmanagerial employees) working in technical roles may provide a conduit for developing greater trust between the organizations. It may also provide an

---

[1] Office of the Director of National Intelligence, *Annual Threat Assessment of the US Intelligence Community*, Washington, D.C., April 9, 2021.

[2] White House, *Interim National Security Strategic Guidance*, Washington, D.C., March 2021.

opportunity for individual contributors to discover how their talents and expertise can contribute to solving DoD's and the nation's problems.

Discuss the Details

According to the survey results, few Silicon Valley engineers have personal experience with military life, and most do not inherently trust the military to act in ways with which they would be comfortable. In addition, the results also indicate that how DoD uses AI influences the respondents' level of comfort with that application or use. Many engineers and software developers work on systems and applications that are complex and involve detailed information. Therefore, it is plausible to assume that many of these individuals recognize that the battlefield can be a complex environment and that there are nuances and corner cases to consider when thinking about how DoD will use AI. An area for further investigation would be exploring the potential benefits of DoD engaging Silicon Valley engineers and software developers on some of the details of how it intends to use AI and how the military is considering the nuanced and complex situations in which it would be used. This shared understanding could provide a foundation for expanding trust between DoD and Silicon Valley employees, prevent misinformation or misconceptions from filling in the gaps in information on the part of engineers and software developers, and reassure the community that DoD is working through how AI-enabled technologies can be used ethically and responsibly.

Discuss Shared Values

Another area for further exploration is investigating opportunities for DoD and Silicon Valley employees to engage over shared values and principles. The five DoD ethical principles for AI could potentially serve as the beginning of the conversation with leading Silicon Valley engineers and software developers regarding DoD uses of AI to better understand the extent and limits of those shared values. Discussions could potentially include use cases for AI that DoD would be uncomfortable with. Many Silicon Valley Employees respondents were uncomfortable with allowing AI to use lethal force without human supervision, a concern many respondents working in the DIB also share. DoD policy explicitly recognizes that decisions about the potential use of lethal force require appropriate human judgment and control. DoD's recently released ethical framework for the use of AI is based on its desire to cultivate a workforce that would be deeply uncomfortable with some potential uses of AI and would raise questions when appropriate to ensure that its use of AI remains consistent with its ethical principles[3] and with the values of the American people. Discussing these specifics might help reassure some private sector technology workers that DoD shares their values about how AI should be used and that they can trust the military to use AI in a way that they will be comfortable with.

Expose Technology Workers to the Realities of Military Life

Since the establishment of the all-volunteer force during the Vietnam era, fewer and fewer Americans have experienced the reality of military service or have close ties with those who do serve.[4] The data from this survey show that this fact is particularly true of software engineers working for cutting-edge AI firms. Con-

---

[3] DoD, "DOD Adopts Ethical Principles for Artificial Intelligence," press release, February 24, 2020.

[4] Amy Schafer, *Generations of War*, Washington, D.C.: Center for a New American Security, May 8, 2017.

sequently, these individuals have little understanding of the operational routines of the military, whether in wartime or in peacetime, and the opportunities they have to make a meaningful impact on the daily lives of service members. Another area for possible future investigation would be to explore the potential benefit of expanding opportunities to expose the United States' most innovative and experienced AI experts to how DoD does things today so that they can imagine how the department could do things better tomorrow.

Survey Methodology

Sample Size and Precision

The primary analysis includes estimation of means (the average value across a group of survey responses), proportions (the ratio of respondents who provided a particular response compared with the whole group), margin of error (MoE) (how closely a survey result likely reflects the true population value), and 95-percent confidence intervals (the range of values that have a 95-percent probability of containing the true mean for a population, another indicator of the precision of the mean value) for the survey items. The research team also computed independent survey estimates for the different samples from the three distinct survey populations (i.e., Silicon Valley Employees, DIB, and Alumni of Top CS Universities). In addition, they estimated minimum detectable differences in comparisons of any two groups, using the final sample sizes. This appendix reports the MoE, as an indicator of precision, for the final sample sizes of respondents in each population. Calculations were conducted for binary variables, with assumed prevalence of 0.50 (50 percent), which yields the most-conservative precision (with largest variance at 50 percent) and also 0.10 (10 percent). The analyses found that the sample sizes of 726, 200, and 252 survey completions in Table 3.2 yield an MoE of 3.6 percent, 6.9 percent, and 6.0 percent, respectively, under prevalence of 50 percent. When prevalence is either 10 percent or 90 percent, the MoE for the three sample sizes (726, 200, 252) is 2.2 percent, 4.2 percent, and 3.7 percent, respectively.

Also, the researchers estimated the minimum detectable differences (or difference in two proportions) for each pair of populations of the sizes of the respondent populations. For two populations or groups of sample sizes 252 (Alumni of Top CS Universities) and 200 (DIB), the minimum detectable difference is 13.8 percent. That is, if a response is chosen by an estimated 50 percent of one group, 63.8 percent or more of the second group would have to have chosen that response (difference greater than or equal to 14 percent) to yield a statistically significant difference. The second comparison used the Silicon Valley Employees sample (726) and the DIB (200). In this case, the minimum detectable difference is 11.7 percent (a difference between 50 percent and 61.7 percent).

The calculations suggest that the minimum detectable differences also represent practically significant or meaningful differences. It should also be noted that although the MoE is smallest and has the best precision for the group with the largest sample size, the MoE for a comparison of survey estimates (proportions) between two groups is often constrained by the smaller of the two sample sizes. Finally, hypothetical calculations were conducted with binary variables, as these tend to result in more-conservative calculations of minimum detectable difference than do calculations conducted with continuous measures.

Sample Representativeness

Recruiting survey respondents could contribute to potential response bias, especially when the survey topic is controversial and could result in systematic nonresponse. To assess the degree of response bias, the study team first tabulated the universe of potential respondents, using the Insights tool provided by Seekout.io, a firm that provides analytics to assist with the recruitment of software engineers. These tabulations provided breakdowns of the potential respondent pool by geographic location, gender, technical discipline, and years of work experience. The study team then monitored the sample characteristics while the survey was in the field so that the study recruitment could be adjusted to compensate for observed variations between the universe (underlying population) and the demographic characteristics of actual survey respondents.[1]

Despite these efforts to monitor and reduce systematic nonresponse, the nature of the survey topic remained a significant potential contributor to bias. There are three reasons for this. First, given that this study was funded by DoD, it is possible that individuals strongly opposed to DoD might boycott the survey because of a distrust of how the results would be used or an objection to assisting DoD in any way. Second, it is possible that individuals who strongly objected to any cooperation with DoD might also attempt to disproportionately register their objections in an attempt to persuade their employers to avoid any future involvement with DoD. That is, the direction of the bias would not be known a priori. Third, the survey topic might have disproportionately recruited software engineers with an above-average level of interest in the U.S. military and global affairs.

Despite the challenges of getting a sample to be representative of the underlying population of interest, the tabulations suggested that the survey participants from Silicon Valley companies (Google, Microsoft, and Amazon) reasonably matched the demographics of the target population. For example, on the key dimension of position type, shown in Figure A.1, the proportions of software engineers, other engineers, and nonengineers were roughly equal in the survey responses and target population (well within the MoE): 81 percent of respondents were software engineers, compared with 77 percent in the target population; 10 percent of respondents were other technical staff, such as product managers, testers, or Dev/Ops engineers, compared with 12 percent in the target population; and 8 percent of respondents were nonengineers, compared with 11 percent of the population.[2] This analysis suggested that the study sample adequately represents the underlying population.

Survey Demographics

To evaluate the representativeness of the study sample, the researchers compared demographic characteristics among survey respondents and the underlying population—that is, all people in the data sources from which survey respondents were selected. The researcher team described the sample along five demographic characteristics: gender, state of residence, years of experience, educational degree obtained, and job discipline. In general, the research found that the sample is representative. Table A.1 shows the differences in several demographic characteristics between the universe of potential survey respondents and the actual respondents to the survey.

---

[1] For more information about Seekout.io's Insight tool, see SeekOut, "Searching with SeekOut: People Insights," webpage, undated. This tool was used to understand the demographics of all three survey populations to better understand whether the survey sample was reflective of the overall universe of potential survey participants.

[2] For two reasons, the researchers sought to recruit participants who represented a variety of job disciplines only from the Silicon Valley Employees population. First, they wanted to include technical employees who were not software engineers—such as product managers, testers, and site reliability engineers—in the RAND sample, since, in Silicon Valley corporations, these jobs frequently require software engineering knowledge but often do not require a software engineering background in other firms. Second, we sought to recruit a small number of nontechnical employees from Silicon Valley corporations, because some individuals with a nontechnical background have played a significant role in employee activism at these companies. The analysis indicated that there was not a statistically meaningful difference between these employees and other employees in the Silicon Valley Employees population.

FIGURE A.1

Silicon Valley Employees, by Position Type

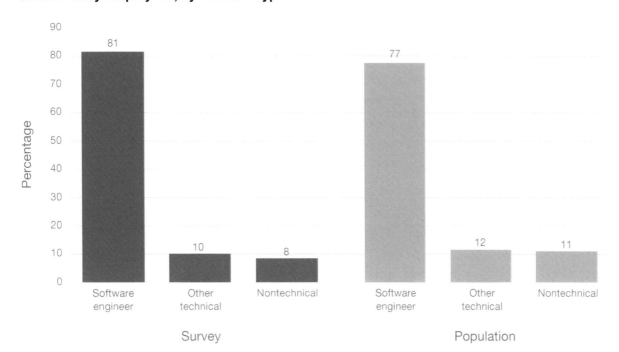

Geographic Representation

The Silicon Valley Employees population and sample were disproportionately located in California and Washington state, reflecting the locations of Microsoft, Google, and Amazon headquarters. In both groups (population and sample), roughly 45 percent of employees were in Washington and 35 percent were in California. Both also had roughly 10 percent of employees in New York, with the rest scattered among other locations.

Both the Alumni of Top CS Universities population and corresponding sample were predominantly in California, New York, Texas, and Washington state. In both cases, more than 35 percent were in California. Of the top five locations for each group, those four states overlapped; however, Georgia ranked in the top five for the target population, but not for the sample, and Massachusetts ranked in the top five for the sample but not the target population (Table A.1).

The DIB was less concentrated geographically. Roughly 25 percent of the population and sample were still in California, but other locations also had large numbers of employees, including Colorado, the Washington, D.C., metro area (including Virginia and Maryland), as well as Texas, Florida, and New York. The biggest geographic difference between the sample and target population was the survey's overrepresentation of employees in Texas.

Years of Work Experience

The majority of both the sample and target populations—more than 50 percent—had more than ten years of experience.

Respondents from the Silicon Valley Employees population with more than ten years of experience were the majority: almost 60 percent for the population and just under 50 percent for the sample. Both had roughly the same number of people with six to ten years of experience and under two years; however, in the sample, those with two to five years were overrepresented. The proportion of Alumni of Top CS Universities respondents with two to five years and six to ten years of experience also were very similar between the two popula-

TABLE A.1

Comparison of Survey Respondents with Universe of Potential Survey Respondents

Characteristic	Silicon Valley Employees		DIB		Top CS Univ. Alumni	
	Survey Respondent	Target Population	Survey Respondents	Target Population	Survey Respondents	Target Population
State or U.S. Territory						
California	33.4%	34.7%	15.9%	23.9%	26.8%	35.8%
Washington	39.0%	43.8%	0.5%	4.4%	11.8%	11.0%
Virginia-Maryland-D.C.	1.6%	1.2%	18.1%	17.7%	4.1%	1.8%
New York	9.9%	7.9%	8.2%	6.0%	7.7%	9.3%
Massachusetts	4.2%	1.8%	7.7%	4.6%	9.4%	5.0%
Other	11.9%	10.4%	49.5%	43.4%	40.2%	37.0%
Education						
Less than bachelor's degree	4.8%	5.3%	2.4%	14.5%	2.7%	5.1%
Bachelor's degree	51.5%	49.6%	59.6%	54.7%	35.0%	37.4%
Master's degree	31.2%	36.9%	31.9%	29.2%	39.0%	42.5%
Ph.D.	12.5%	8.2%	6.0%	1.6%	23.3%	15.1%
Years of Experience						
Less than 2 years	3.7%	5.7%	7.4%	8.1%	3.4%	17.2%
2 to 5 years	23.9%	11.9%	14.9%	16.9%	16.0%	12.7%
6 to 10	24.3%	25.1%	18.9%	18.8%	18.6%	17.4%
More than 10	48.2%	57.3%	56.1%	56.1%	52.0%	51.3%

tions: Alumni of Top CS Universities participants with less than two years of experience were slightly underrepresented in the sample.

Silicon Valley Employees respondents with more than ten years of experience were the majority: almost 60 percent for the population and just under 50 percent for the sample. Both had roughly the same number of people with six to ten years of experience and under two years; however, in the sample, those with two to five years were overrepresented.

The target DIB population and sample also had very similar lengths of work experience. Like the Alumni of Top CS Universities and Silicon Valley Employees populations, those with more than ten years of experience were the majority.

Educational Attainment

In both the sample and target Alumni of Top CS Universities populations, most individuals had master's degrees as their highest level of educational attainment.

The education levels of the Silicon Valley Employees sample were similar to those of the target population, with one-half reporting bachelor's degrees as the highest level of education; around one-third reported master's degrees, and one-tenth had doctorates.

Education levels between the groups of DIB employees were similar, with the exception that the survey underrepresented those with less than a bachelor's degree.

Gender Distribution

At the Silicon Valley companies, men outnumber women substantially in the target population and sample, but men were overrepresented in the sample, making up 80 percent of the sample compared with 75 percent of the population.

The target DIB population and sample were very similar with respect to the distribution of gender: Like the Alumni of Top CS Universities and Silicon Valley Employees populations, the majority were men.

Respondent Perspectives on Department of Defense

Open-ended responses and any additional comments that respondents provided at the end of the survey were used to further elucidate respondents' views regarding DoD and to help verify that respondents expressed a variety of views on DoD, and that no particular opinion (i.e., favorable or unfavorable) was absent. If few or no responses suggested either favorable or unfavorable predispositions toward DoD, one could surmise that respondents with a particular viewpoint or perspective on these issues boycotted the survey or did not reveal their true disposition. The results suggest that that was not the case for this survey. Although the precise ratio of favorable to unfavorable views about DoD across the survey populations cannot be known, it can at least be assumed that there is a distribution and variation of views expressed and no unanimous (or single) viewpoint. This survey revealed a range in respondents' support for DoD's use of AI, confirming that the survey responses reflected many different perspectives on these issues.

The survey included five open-ended questions. Most respondents answered some of these open-ended prompts (82.4 percent answered at least one), while more than a quarter of the respondents answered all of them (28.8 percent). Some findings from the open-ended responses suggest that respondents represent a variety of implicit ideologies. Across employer groups, there were respondents who held unequivocally strong views both in favor and not in favor of DoD's use of AI, according to Figure A.2. Each respondent's answers were manually reviewed and coded to determine whether or not the respondents had unequivocally "Favorable," "Neutral/Unclear," or "Unfavorable" positions on DoD's use of AI. The analytic methodology is described later in this appendix.

Analytic Methods

Statistical Analysis of Responses to Multiple-Choice Questions

The quantitative analysis involved estimation of means and proportions for individual survey items. Most survey items in the questionnaire used a Likert-scale-type response to elicit the range of responses. For example, the team assessed degree of trust using a five-point response scale with these levels: a great deal, quite a lot, some, very little, and none. They also assessed degree of comfort with applications of AI in certain contexts using a five-point response scale with levels very comfortable, somewhat comfortable, neutral, somewhat uncomfortable, and very uncomfortable. In preliminary analysis, the researchers summarized the responses for each item using mean, standard deviation, five-point summary, and computed frequency listings. Because of the possibility of nonsymmetric distributions, the team created a full breakdown of the endorsements of the different response levels using proportions (or the full distribution) and graphical visualizations. To compare responses with a single item between two samples (Silicon Valley Employees, DIB) or responses to two items within the same sample (Silicon Valley Employees), the researchers used Cohen's definition of effect size to assess whether

FIGURE A.2

Respondents' Support for Department of Defense Use of Artificial Intelligence, by Employer

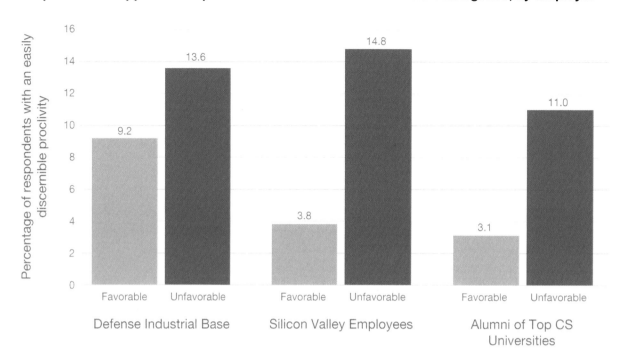

differences in the standard deviation(s) and range of responses of each item constituted a "medium" or "large" effect size.[3] Only responses that could be considered a "medium" or "large" effect size were interpreted as a practically significant (i.e., meaningful) difference. When conducting regressions, the researchers conducted only one significance test and thus did not correct for performing multiple tests.

To investigate inter-item correlation, the researchers created correlograms for all questions in a subgroup. A correlogram visualizes the correlation across questions using a matrix, where each cell is (or represents) the numerical correlation coefficient. Correlations were not common across questions, with a few key exceptions. Responses to questions about lethal use of AI were highly correlated with one another but not with other AI-related questions. For the trust in groups section, responses for the three questions that refer to "civil servants" were correlated. In the war justification section, the three scenarios about an American adversary engaging a neighboring nation were correlated. However, these were the exceptions to the rule, and, in general, responses were not correlated.

Methods of Regression Analysis for Multiple-Choice Questions

One important aspect of analyzing the multiple-choice questions was determining which characteristics of the population correlated with the greatest variation in responses. Without this analysis, analyzing the data by a particular characteristic—for example, the survey population or the age of the respondent—might appear to be significant, but the results might be less impactful than analysis by a different characteristic. For example, members of the DIB survey population, on average, are older than are respondents from the other two populations; consequently, differences in survey responses that initially appear to be correlated with survey population may be better explained by variations in the age of the survey respondents. To consider which characteristics of the survey participants had the greatest statistical significance on survey responses, the

---

3   Jacob Cohen, *Statistical Power Analysis for the Behavioral Sciences*, 2nd ed., New York: Academic Press, 1988.

researchers used regression models with potential confounding variables—such as gender, age, or personal connections to the armed services—to see which variables had the strongest impact on survey responses.

The model used was a multivariate ordinal logistic regression. The model is multivariate because it contains the variables that the researchers thought could potentially influence survey responses: population, gender, age, military connection, years in industry, and region. Regressions should be parsimonious, meaning that variables should be omitted if they either (1) have questionable relevance to the dependent variable (the survey response) or (2) correlate with an existing variable while adding no new explanatory power (such as having both age and college graduation year). This is why some variables available from the survey were not included, such as whether one had served in the military, which correlates with whether a family member served in the military.

To model population, binary variables were created for the Alumni of Top CS Universities and Silicon Valley Employees populations. These variables measure the difference between Alumni of Top CS Universities and Silicon Valley Employees respondents and those in the DIB. When using factor variables, one factor is always left out to serve as the base from which there is a distinction. DIB was picked as the default, as the goal was to see how perspectives differed for those in the other two populations. Similarly, binary variables were created for two geographic regions—California and Washington state, and New York and New Jersey— to investigate whether there could be a geographic component driving attitudes.

Logistic regressions are used when the dependent variable is not a continuous variable, such as age in years. A typical logistic regression is on a binary variable, such as whether or not someone chose to go to college. The ordinal logistic model used in this analysis measures the log of the probability that an independent variable moves the dependent ordinal variable up or down its ranking.

This model was preferred over other more-common regression models because of the nature of the data. The survey responses (e.g., very comfortable, somewhat comfortable, neutral, somewhat uncomfortable, and very uncomfortable) are noninterval variables. Although ranked, the intervals between them are not quantifiable: The gap between very comfortable and somewhat comfortable is not necessarily comparable with the one between somewhat comfortable and neutral. Such noninterval data violate the assumptions used in an ordinary least squares regression. Another logistic regression, the multinomial logistic regression, is also inappropriate given the ranked nature of the survey data. A multinomial logistic regression assumes that the differences in the outcomes have no order, such as categorical variables for race, and thus loses all the information in the rank of the survey responses.

The output of these regressions does not include p-values and instead uses t-values. P-values can be calculated from the t-values if one assumes that the sample size is large enough to use the assumption of infinite degrees of freedom. Another common output of interest with ordinal logistic regressions is an odds ratio. These were not calculated for this output because the goal was primarily to determine whether there was a statistically significant impact of the independent variables on survey responses. The odds ratio can be easily calculated by exponentiating the coefficients in the "value" columns.

Methods of Analysis for the Open-Ended Questions

The data from the open-ended questions were intended to identify themes among certain populations of respondents or to reveal patterns across groups. To achieve this, conceptual content analysis was primarily used for reviewing the open-ended survey responses. For this study, the open-ended responses were analyzed using (1) frequency counts for specific words (e.g., *drone*) or collocates (e.g., *SolarWinds*) throughout the textual data in the survey responses, and (2) more-implicit and interpretive analysis of respondents' perceptions (e.g., if and when DoD should leverage AI to achieve its objectives) to elicit further respondent characteristics.

Prior to conducting frequency counts, text data were cleaned to identify any potentially unreliable and invalid responses (e.g., "Wouldn't you like to know, Fed Boy?") or to reconcile differences in spelling or correct spelling errors (e.g., from "Ben Laden" to "Bin Laden"). After a preliminary manual read of responses, deliberate Boolean keyword searches helped count keywords that were identified as prevalent themes throughout the response set. This process was iterative; as multiple alternatives to a particular response were identified (e.g., "NYT," "New York Times," and "NY Times"), ongoing cleaning and coercing the data set yielded better searches and more-reliable word frequencies.

Conceptual analysis can also be leveraged to yield more-implicit findings from survey responses. In this instance, responses were coded to assess respondents' propensity to support DoD's use of AI. As with most content analysis, this was an inherently subjective and manual process. Each respondent's answers were reviewed to determine whether the respondents appeared ideologically and unequivocally "Favorable," "Neutral/Unclear," or "Unfavorable" toward DoD's use of AI. Responses were coded as "Neutral/Unclear" when there were either no open-ended responses or the available answers were inconclusive. For respondents with particularly complicated responses that seemed more explicitly event-specific and whose responses included both "Favorable" and "Unfavorable" considerations, these were coded "Other." These codes were adjudicated between two researchers for inter-rater reliability and, following initial codes, were reviewed against their multiple-choice responses to check for consistency. Table A.2 has examples of some quotes from respondents that helped inform how they should be coded. These codes were then used to characterize respondents and, where appropriate, were used as the basis for subgroup analysis for other survey questions.

Definitions and Estimates for Survey Populations

Silicon Valley Employees

Eligibility for recruitment was defined on the basis of current employer—specifically, if current employer is

- Microsoft
- Google
- Amazon or Amazon Web Services (and job functions are not warehouse operations).

The researchers estimated that this population comprises approximately 450,000 individuals.[4]

Alumni of Top Ranked Computer Science Universities

Eligibility for this population was achieved if an individual met the following three criteria:

- Attended Stanford University, Massachusetts Institute of Technology; Carnegie Mellon University; Carnegie Mellon University School of Computer Science; University of California, Berkeley; UC Berkeley Electrical Engineering & Computer Sciences (EECS); University of Illinois at Urbana-Champaign; Cornell University; University of Washington; Georgia Institute of Technology; The University of Texas at Austin; or the University of Michigan
- Received a degree (bachelor's, master's, or doctorate) in CS
- Current employer is not Google, Microsoft, or Amazon.

---

[4] See Macrotrends, "Alphabet: Number of Employees 2006–2021/GOOG," webpage, undated-a; and Macrotrends, "Microsoft: Number of Employees 2006–2021/MSFT," webpage, undated-b. We assume that Amazon has a similar number of corporate and technical employees as the other two companies.

TABLE A.2

Example of Responses from Open Text Fields in Survey Instrument

Code	Detail or Quote Example	Proportion of Respondents
Favorable	"AI should be used in basically any situation where it might give the US an advantage over foreign powers." "I believe in the necessity for the US to complete in the AI 'arms' race" "The use of AI in the military is critical for the US to maintain a dominant role" "We need to make sure we are ahead of our adversaries in the research and development of AI." "If we do not employ [sic] AI in our military then we would likely see a scenario where we were not the capable on the battlefield."	4.6%
Neutral/ Unclear	"AI, like other technology, is a double-edged tool . . ." "AI working perfectly is a relative term." "DoD needs significant civilian oversight for ethics [sic] including an independent review board."	79.2%
Unfavorable	"I would never trust the military in anything it does" "The military should never have control of AI." "The US military cannot be trusted to use AI technology . . . " "[M]ost or all of the US presidents since the 1960s could be charged with war crimes based on the Nuremberg laws." "[AI] is a waste of resources in the context of humans vs. global warming"	13.8%
Other	"I'm mostly fine with AI development, but human-in-the-loop for actually firing weapons I think is important (with a notable of exception for intercepting missiles or other defensive actions where a human is too slow). AGI risk (MIRI style goal alignment problem) I think is also real . . ." "AI should be utilized solely with a human-in-the-loop . . ." "AI is a tool which should be monitored and controlled by humans with a moral compass." "AI is a useful tool but cannot eliminate accountability. Safeguards need to be designed to maintain accountability." "AI may be used for primarily defensive applications but should not be used for primarily offensive applications."	2.4%

The researchers estimate that there are approximately 300,000 individuals who meet all of these three criteria.[5]

The Defense Industrial Base

Eligibility for this population was achieved if an individual met the following two criteria:

- Current employer is Lockheed Martin, Leidos, Booz Allen Hamilton, Northrop Grumman, Raytheon, SAIC, BAE Systems, United Technologies, Rockwell Collins, L3Harris Technologies, or Palantir; or if current employer is Boeing and employee has an active security clearance.[6]

---

[5]   To calculate this estimate, the team reviewed the statistics published by each college as to the number of graduates from their CS department for any years such statistics were available. In many cases, these colleges also provide self-reported statistics about which employers their students will be working for upon graduation. Using these data, the team estimated that approximately 1,000 graduates from each college annually work for employers not contained in either the DIB or Silicon Valley Employees populations. Additionally, the team assumed that an average software engineer remains in the workforce for approximately 30 years. Varying these assumptions would alter the estimated size of this population proportionately.

[6]   The researchers selected these companies because they had the largest number of software engineers available in RAND data sources who also indicated that they held a security clearance.

- Current job title is software engineer, Java software engineer, lead software engineer, staff software engineer, software engineering manager, associate software engineer, principal staff software engineer, senior Java software engineer, lead principal software engineer, senior software engineer, senior staff software engineer, principal software engineer, software test engineer, or senior principal software engineer.

The research team estimated that approximately 50,000 individuals meet these criteria.[7]

---

[7] Estimate based on information from LinkedIn company profile pages.

Survey Instrument

Exploring Views About the Use of Artificial Intelligence

SECTION A. These questions ask about hypothetical U.S. Department of Defense projects that use Artificial Intelligence (AI).

1. **Please indicate how comfortable you would find it to employ Artificial Intelligence (AI) for each of the following. Assume for each of the cases that the AI works and achieves the intended goal.**

	Very Comfortable	Somewhat Comfortable	Neutral	Somewhat Uncomfortable	Very Uncomfortable
a. Using AI to identify enemy soldiers and vehicles and allowing it to fire weapons to eliminate them.	☐	☐	☐	☐	☐
b. Using AI supervised by American soldiers to make a recommendation about how to best eliminate enemy soldiers and vehicles.	☐	☐	☐	☐	☐
c. Using AI to locate terrorists operating outside the United States for the purpose of eliminating them.	☐	☐	☐	☐	☐
d. Using AI to enhance the United States' military strength to ensure it remains in a dominant position relative to its enemies.	☐	☐	☐	☐	☐
e. Using AI to reduce civilian casualties and collateral damage to humanitarian targets, such as hospitals, by more precisely targeting enemy soldiers.	☐	☐	☐	☐	☐

	Very Comfortable	Somewhat Comfortable	Neutral	Somewhat Uncomfortable	Very Uncomfortable
f. Using AI to save the lives of U.S soldiers by firing on enemy soldiers before they do harm.	☐	☐	☐	☐	☐
g. Using AI to improve the ability of robots to disable enemy explosives.	☐	☐	☐	☐	☐
h. Using AI to intercept and destroy unmanned enemy weapon systems on the battlefield, such as missiles, that move too quickly for humans to intervene.	☐	☐	☐	☐	☐
i. Using AI to create unmanned medical evacuation helicopters to retrieve injured soldiers from the battlefield.	☐	☐	☐	☐	☐
j. Using AI to optimize the supply chain flow of weapons, ammunition, and spare parts to the battlefield.	☐	☐	☐	☐	☐
k. Using AI to optimize the supply chain flow of food, medical supplies, and fuel to the battlefield.	☐	☐	☐	☐	☐
l. Using AI to audit the U.S. military's financial transactions to improve transparency and identify waste.	☐	☐	☐	☐	☐
m. Using AI to help the U.S. military assist the victims of natural disasters, such as hurricanes or earthquakes.	☐	☐	☐	☐	☐

* Note: the order of these questions will be randomized.

Section B. This question does not involve the U.S. military.

2. **Please indicate how comfortable you would find it to employ Artificial Intelligence (AI) in the following scenario. Assume for this case that the AI works and achieves the intended goal.**

	Very Comfortable	Somewhat Comfortable	Neutral	Somewhat Uncomfortable	Very Uncomfortable
a. Using AI to help humanitarian non-governmental organizations, such as Doctors Without Borders, assist the victims of natural disasters, such as hurricanes or earthquakes.	☐	☐	☐	☐	☐

NOTE: This question does not involve the U.S. military.

Section C. This question does not involve the use of Artificial Intelligence.

3. **Please indicate how comfortable you would find it to assist in a project intended to achieve the following goal.**

	Very Comfortable	Somewhat Comfortable	Neutral	Somewhat uncomfortable	Very Uncomfortable
a. Without using AI, help the U.S. military prevent the use of AI by enemy militaries.	☐	☐	☐	☐	☐

SECTION D. This section contains questions about your trust in various institutions in society, the government, and your own workplace.

4. **How much do you trust each of the following institutions to act in a way that you agree with?**

	A Great Deal	Quite a Lot	Some	Very Little	None
a. The U.S. federal government	☐	☐	☐	☐	☐
b. The U.S. military	☐	☐	☐	☐	☐
c. U.S. Intelligence Agencies, such as the CIA or NSA	☐	☐	☐	☐	☐
d. U.S. technology companies, such as Facebook, Apple, Amazon, Netflix, Google, or Microsoft	☐	☐	☐	☐	☐
e. The U.S. medical system	☐	☐	☐	☐	☐
f. U.S. Colleges and Universities	☐	☐	☐	☐	☐
g. The media, such as newspapers, TV, and radio	☐	☐	☐	☐	☐
h. Your employer or company	☐	☐	☐	☐	☐

NOTE: the order of these questions will be randomized

5. **For each of the following groups, how much do you trust them to act in a way that you agree with?**

	A Great Deal	Quite a Lot	Some	Very Little	None
a. Political appointees leading U.S. federal agencies	☐	☐	☐	☐	☐
b. U.S. elected officials holding a federal position (e.g., congressman)	☐	☐	☐	☐	☐
c. Uniformed military officers in the U.S. Military	☐	☐	☐	☐	☐
d. Career civil servants working at the U.S. Department of Defense	☐	☐	☐	☐	☐
e. Career civil servants working at U.S. intelligence agencies	☐	☐	☐	☐	☐
f. Career civil servants working at other non-defense U.S. government agencies	☐	☐	☐	☐	☐
g. Software engineers working at U.S. technology companies	☐	☐	☐	☐	☐
h. Corporate CEOs of U.S. technology companies	☐	☐	☐	☐	☐
i. Doctors and other medical professionals	☐	☐	☐	☐	☐
j. Professors at U.S. Universities and Colleges	☐	☐	☐	☐	☐
k. Journalists at media corporations	☐	☐	☐	☐	☐
l. Fellow employees at your company	☐	☐	☐	☐	☐

NOTE: The order of these questions will be randomized

6. **Please indicate the degree to which you agree or disagree with the following statements about your workplace.**

	Strongly Agree	Agree	Neither Agree nor Disagree	Disagree	Strongly Disagree
a. People are expected to follow their own personal and moral beliefs in their work.	☐	☐	☐	☐	☐
b. It is very important to follow strictly the company's rules and procedures.	☐	☐	☐	☐	☐
c. People protect their own interest above other considerations.	☐	☐	☐	☐	☐
d. The effect of decisions on the public is a primary concern in my company.	☐	☐	☐	☐	☐
e. People are expected to do anything to further the company's interests.	☐	☐	☐	☐	☐
f. People are very concerned about what is generally best for the employees in the company.	☐	☐	☐	☐	☐
g. In my company, each person is expected, above all, to work efficiently.	☐	☐	☐	☐	☐
h. Decisions in my company are primarily viewed in terms of contribution to profit.	☐	☐	☐	☐	☐

NOTE: The order of these questions will be randomized.

SECTION E. The questions in this section ask about real-world events and activities that have shaped your impressions of the U.S. Defense Department. Please list any such events in the text box that follows each question.

7. Please name one or two past events or news stories that have influenced your expectations of whether the U.S. military would use Artificial Intelligence based software products in an acceptable way. Please do not include any personally identifiable information in your response.

1) _____

2) _____

8. Please name one or two past events and news stories that have influenced your expectations about what the U.S. military would use Artificial Intelligence for. Please do not include any personally identifiable information in your response.

1) _____

2) _____

SECTION F. The questions in this section involve the current state of the world and potential threats to the United States.

9. Below is a list of potential threats to the interests of the U.S. in the next 10 years. For each, please indicate if you see this as a critical threat, an important but not critical threat, a moderate threat, or not an important threat at all.

	A critical threat	An important but not critical threat	A moderate threat	Not an important threat at all	Don't know/ prefer not to say
a. Nuclear weapon attacks	☐	☐	☐	☐	☐
b. International terrorist attacks	☐	☐	☐	☐	☐
c. Cyberattacks	☐	☐	☐	☐	☐
d. Armed conflicts between nations	☐	☐	☐	☐	☐
e. Armed conflicts within nations	☐	☐	☐	☐	☐
f. Global climate change	☐	☐	☐	☐	☐
g. International financial instability	☐	☐	☐	☐	☐
h. Rising military capabilities in potentially hostile foreign countries	☐	☐	☐	☐	☐

NOTE: the order of these questions will be randomized

10. **Would you say that the following represent a very serious threat to the United States, a moderately serious threat, just a slight threat, or no threat at all?**

	Very Serious Threat to the United States	Moderately Serious Threat to the United States	Just a Slight Threat to the United States	No Threat At All to the United States	Don't Know/Prefer Not To Say
a. North Korea	☐	☐	☐	☐	☐
b. Russia	☐	☐	☐	☐	☐
c. China	☐	☐	☐	☐	☐
d. Iran	☐	☐	☐	☐	☐

NOTE: The order of these questions will be randomized.

SECTION G. This section describes a variety of hypothetical world events.

11. **Please indicate how justified you think the United States would be in using military force in response to each of the following events.**

	Justified	Somewhat Justified	Neutral	Somewhat Unjustified	Unjustified
a. A foreign government has attacked American territory and killed American civilians.	☐	☐	☐	☐	☐
b. A U.S. Navy ship has been attacked and American sailors have been killed.	☐	☐	☐	☐	☐
c. An American adversary has invaded and seized populated territory from a neighboring nation.	☐	☐	☐	☐	☐
d. An American adversary has invaded and seized unpopulated territory, such as a small island, from a neighboring nation.	☐	☐	☐	☐	☐
e. An American adversary has invaded and forcibly changed the government of a neighboring nation.	☐	☐	☐	☐	☐
f. To protect an oppressed population from abuses committed by their government.	☐	☐	☐	☐	☐
g. To break an economic embargo an American adversary is using to coerce another nation.	☐	☐	☐	☐	☐
h. To defend a NATO ally which has requested assistance against foreign aggression.	☐	☐	☐	☐	☐

	Justified	Somewhat Justified	Neutral	Somewhat Unjustified	Unjustified
i. To defend a non-NATO ally, such as Saudi Arabia or the Philippines, which has requested assistance against foreign aggression.	☐	☐	☐	☐	☐
j. To uphold the requirements of an international treaty.	☐	☐	☐	☐	☐
k. To enforce a UN resolution.	☐	☐	☐	☐	☐
l. To preempt an expected attack by an adversary on American soldiers deployed abroad.	☐	☐	☐	☐	☐

NOTE: The order of these questions will be randomized.

SECTION H. The questions in this section ask about how you interact with mass media, such as news, television, radio, and websites, among other sources. Please read each question carefully and select the most appropriate response for each item.

12. **In general, how much trust and confidence do you have in the mass media—such as newspapers, TV, and radio—when it comes to reporting the news fully, accurately, and fairly?**
    - ☐ A great deal
    - ☐ A fair amount
    - ☐ Not very much
    - ☐ None at all

13. **Please indicate how often you get your news about current events, world affairs, and science and technology developments from the following sources.**

	Every Day	Several Times per Week	Occasionally	Never
a. Websites of news organizations	☐	☐	☐	☐
b. Podcasts	☐	☐	☐	☐
c. Blogs	☐	☐	☐	☐
d. Social media sites	☐	☐	☐	☐
e. Print newspapers	☐	☐	☐	☐
f. Television	☐	☐	☐	☐
g. Radio	☐	☐	☐	☐
h. Print news magazines	☐	☐	☐	☐
j. Discussions with your friends and family	☐	☐	☐	☐

14. **Please indicate the two sources you rely on the most for news about current events, world affairs, and science and technology developments.**

1) _____

2) _____

15. **SECTION I. Demographic Information**

16. **What is your age?**

    ____years old

17. **What is your gender?**
    - ☐ Male
    - ☐ Female
    - ☐ Prefer not to say

18. **In what state or U.S. territory do you live?**

    _____

19. **What is the highest degree or level of school you have completed?**
    - ☐ Did not finish high school
    - ☐ High school diploma or GED
    - ☐ Some college or 2-year degree
    - ☐ Bachelor's degree

☐ Master's degree
☐ Doctorate degree

20. **Have you ever served in the armed forces of the United States?**
    ☐ Yes, currently on active duty
    ☐ Yes, currently in National Guard or Reserves
    ☐ Yes, retired
    ☐ Yes, separated or discharged
    ☐ Never served in the U.S. armed forces

21. **Have you ever served in the armed forces of another country?**
    ☐ Yes, currently on active duty
    ☐ Yes, currently in National Guard or Reserves
    ☐ Yes, retired
    ☐ Yes, separated or discharged
    ☐ Never served in the U.S. armed forces of another country

22. **Which of the following people, if any, served in the military of any country? Please select all that apply.**
    ☐ My father
    ☐ My mother
    ☐ My sibling
    ☐ My spouse or significant other
    ☐ Other person/people close to me
    ☐ None

23. **What is your job type or discipline?**
    ☐ Software Developer
    ☐ Program Management
    ☐ Test / Quality Assurance (QA)
    ☐ Operations
    ☐ Research
    ☐ Sales
    ☐ Marketing
    ☐ Recruiting
    ☐ Legal
    ☐ Finance
    ☐ Human Resources (HR)
    ☐ Other

24. **What is your management level?**
    ☐ Individual Contributor (not managing the careers of other employees)
    ☐ Lead or Manager (managing a group or team of fewer than 35 people)
    ☐ Executive or Senior Leader (managing a group of 35 people or more)

25. **How many years have you been employed in your current job?**

_____years

26. **How many years have you been employed in the technology industry?**

_____years

27. **Are you employed full time or part time at your current position? If you have more than one position, please think of the one where you work the most hours.**
    - ☐ Full time (35 or more hours per week)
    - ☐ Part time (fewer than 35 hours per week)

28. **If you have other comments or opinions about this topic, please share them here (do not include personally identifiable information.)**

END. Thank you for participating.

Aggregate Survey Results

This appendix lists the number of respondents who selected each option for each item in the survey. In some cases, responses are aggregated to avoid potentially identifying any survey respondents. Responses to open-ended questions are also not provided.

SECTION A. These next questions ask about hypothetical U.S. Department of Defense projects that use Artificial Intelligence (AI).

1. **Please indicate how comfortable you would find it to employ Artificial Intelligence (AI) for each of the following. Assume for each of the cases that the AI works and achieves the intended goal.**

TABLE C.1

Survey Respondents' Comfort Level with Military Use of Artificial Intelligence

	VC	SC	N	SU	VU	NR
a. Using AI to identify enemy soldiers and vehicles and allowing it to fire weapons to eliminate them.	113	123	90	243	619	SV: 2 CS Alum: 0 DIB: 0
b. Using AI supervised by American soldiers to make a recommendation about how to best eliminate enemy soldiers and vehicles.	371	320	141	194	162	SV: 2 CS Alum: 0 DIB: 0
c. Using AI to locate terrorists operating outside the United States for the purpose of eliminating them.	291	245	159	229	264	SV: 2 CS Alum: 0 DIB: 0
d. Using AI to enhance the United States' military strength to ensure it remains in a dominant position relative to its enemies.	381	256	246	144	160	SV: 2 CS Alum: 1 DIB: 0
e. Using AI to reduce civilian casualties and collateral damage to humanitarian targets, such as hospitals, by more precisely targeting enemy soldiers.	368	285	149	214	172	SV: 2 CS Alum: 0 DIB: 0

	VC	SC	N	SU	VU	NR
f. Using AI to save the lives of U.S soldiers by firing on enemy soldiers before they do harm.	147	140	127	286	488	SV: 2 CS Alum: 0 DIB: 0
g. Using AI to improve the ability of robots to disable enemy explosives.	863	226	56	21	21	SV: 3 CS Alum: 0 DIB: 0
h. Using AI to intercept and destroy unmanned enemy weapon systems on the battlefield, such as missiles, that move too quickly for humans to intervene.	641	320	85	84	58	SV: 2 CS Alum: 0 DIB: 0
j. Using AI to create unmanned medical evacuation helicopters to retrieve injured soldiers from the battlefield.	803	251	69	37	28	SV: 2 CS Alum: 0 DIB: 0
k. Using AI to optimize the supply chain flow of weapons, ammunition, and spare parts to the battlefield.	707	236	107	74	63	SV: 3 CS Alum: 0 DIB: 0
l. Using AI to optimize the supply chain flow of food, medical supplies, and fuel to the battlefield.	878	192	56	33	29	SV: 2 CS Alum: 0 DIB: 0
m. Using AI to audit the U.S. military's financial transactions to improve transparency and identify waste.	887	189	63	24	25	SV: 2 CS Alum: 0 DIB: 0
n. Using AI to help the U.S. military assist the victims of natural disasters, such as hurricanes or earthquakes.	913	189	47	20	18	SV: 2 CS Alum: 0 DIB: 1

NOTES: The order of these questions was randomized in the survey. Response scale: very comfortable (VC); somewhat comfortable (SC); neutral (N); somewhat uncomfortable (SU); very uncomfortable (VU); no response (NR).

CS Alum = Alumni of Top CS Universities; SV = Silicon Valley.

Section B. This question does not involve the U.S. military.

2.   Please indicate how comfortable you would find it to employ Artificial Intelligence (AI) in the following scenario. Assume for this case that the AI works and achieves the intended goal.

TABLE C.2
Survey Respondents' Comfort Level with Humanitarian Use of Artificial Intelligence

	VC	SC	N	SU	VU	NR
a. Using AI to help humanitarian non-governmental organizations such as Doctors Without Borders assist the victims of natural disasters such as hurricanes or earthquakes	963	173	26	15	8	SV: 5 CS Alum: 0 DIB: 0

NOTES: Response scale: very comfortable (VC); somewhat comfortable (SC); neutral (N); somewhat uncomfortable (SU); very uncomfortable (VU); no response (NR).

CS Alum = Alumni of Top CS Universities; SV = Silicon Valley.

Section C. This question does not involve the use of Artificial Intelligence.

3.   Please indicate how comfortable you would find it to assist in a project intended to achieve the following goal.

Table C.3. Survey Respondents' Comfort Level with Helping U.S. Military Prevent Enemy Militaries' Use of Artificial Intelligence

	VC	SC	N	SU	VU	NR
b. Without using AI, help the U.S. military prevent the use of AI by enemy militaries.	541	266	254	74	45	SV: 8 CS Alum: 0 DIB: 1

NOTES: Response scale: very comfortable (VC); somewhat comfortable (SC); neutral (N); somewhat uncomfortable (SU); very uncomfortable (VU); no response (NR).

CS Alum = Alumni of Top CS Universities; SV = Silicon Valley.

SECTION D. This section contains questions about your trust in various institutions in society, the government, and your own workplace.

4. How much do you trust each of the following institutions to act in a way that you agree with?

TABLE C.4
Survey Respondents' Trust in Institutions

	GD	Q	S	VL	N	NR
a. The U.S. Federal Government	47	207	584	249	81	SV: 15 CS Alum: 2 DIB: 3
b. The U.S. Military	96	275	450	239	108	SV: 15 CS Alum: 2 DIB: 3
c. U.S. Intelligence Agencies, such as the CIA or NSA	76	227	397	302	166	SV: 15 CS Alum: 2 DIB: 3
d. U.S. technology companies, such as Facebook, Apple, Amazon, Netflix, Google, or Microsoft	68	196	494	300	110	SV: 15 CS Alum: 2 DIB: 3
e. The U.S. medical system	137	318	409	228	76	SV: 15 CS Alum: 2 DIB: 3
f. U.S. Colleges and Universities	197	435	347	138	50	SV: 15 CS Alum: 2 DIB: 4
g. The media, such as newspapers, TV, and radio	36	216	472	293	151	SV: 15 CS Alum: 2 DIB: 3
h. Your employer or company	225	435	382	91	31	SV: 18 CS Alum: 2 DIB: 4

NOTES: The order of these questions was randomized in the survey. Response scale: a great deal (GD); quite a lot (Q); some (S); very little (VL); none (N); no response (NR).

CS Alum = Alumni of Top CS Universities; SV = Silicon Valley.

5.   For each of the following groups, how much do you trust them to act in a way that you agree with?

TABLE C.5
Survey Respondents' Trust in Groups to Act in an Agreeable Way

	GD	Q	S	VL	N	NR
a. Political appointees leading U.S. federal agencies	11	101	495	396	144	SV: 30 CS Alum: 5 DIB: 6
b. U.S. Elected officials holding a federal position (e.g., congressman)	11	67	501	436	132	SV: 30 CS Alum: 5 DIB: 6
c. Uniformed military officers in the U.S. Military	131	367	417	164	68	SV: 30 CS Alum: 5 DIB: 6
d. Career civil servants working at the U.S. Department of Defense	100	391	442	158	55	SV: 31 CS Alum: 5 DIB: 6
e. Career civil servants working at U.S. intelligence agencies	119	337	443	174	74	SV: 30 CS Alum: 5 DIB: 6
f. Career civil servants working at other non-defense U.S. government agencies	159	440	408	108	32	SV: 30 CS Alum: 5 DIB: 6
g. Software engineers working at U.S. technology companies	168	419	440	95	25	SV: 30 CS Alum: 5 DIB: 6
h. Corporate CEOs of U.S. technology companies	33	152	446	351	165	SV: 30 CS Alum: 5 DIB: 6
i. Doctors and other medical professionals	415	518	187	21	5	SV: 30 CS Alum: 5 DIB: 7
j. Professors at U.S. Universities and Colleges	241	488	298	84	36	SV: 30 CS Alum: 5 DIB: 6
k. Journalists at media corporations	64	286	446	227	124	SV: 30 CS Alum: 5 DIB: 6
l. Fellow employees at your company	287	529	285	31	10	SV: 34 CS Alum: 5 DIB: 7

NOTES: The order of these questions was randomized in the survey. Response scale: a great deal (GD); quite a lot (Q); some (S); very little (VL); none (N); no response (NR).

CS Alum = Alumni of Top CS Universities; SV = Silicon Valley.

6. Please indicate the degree to which you agree or disagree with the following statements about your workplace.

TABLE C.6

Role of Ethics in the Respondents' Workplace

	SA	A	N	D	SD	NR
a. People are expected to follow their own personal and moral beliefs in their work.	183	469	311	117	30	SV: 57 CS Alum: 10 DIB: 11
b. It is very important to follow strictly the company's rules and procedures.	203	466	305	117	19	SV: 57 CS Alum: 10 DIB: 11
c. People protect their own interest above other considerations.	98	313	352	290	57	SV: 56 CS Alum: 11 DIB: 11
d. The effect of decisions on the public is a primary concern in my company.	221	440	296	117	37	SV: 57 CS Alum: 10 DIB: 10
e. People are expected to do anything to further the company's interests.	37	121	236	441	275	SV: 58 CS Alum: 9 DIB: 11
f. People are very concerned about what is generally best for the employees in the company.	156	515	284	124	31	SV: 57 CS Alum: 10 DIB: 11
g. In my company, each person is expected, above all, to work efficiently.	167	412	308	191	31	SV: 58 CS Alum: 10 DIB: 11
h. Decisions in my company are primarily viewed in terms of contribution to profit.	113	318	335	277	68	SV: 56 CS Alum: 10 DIB: 11

NOTES: The order of these questions was randomized in the survey. Response scale: strongly agree (SA); agree (A); neither agree nor disagree (N); disagree (D); strongly disagree (SD); no response (NR).

CS Alum = Alumni of Top CS Universities; SV = Silicon Valley.

SECTION F. The questions in this section involve the current state of the world and potential threats to the United States.

7. Below is a list of potential threats to the interests of the U.S. in the next 10 years. For each, please indicate if you see this as a critical threat, an important but not critical threat, a moderate threat, or not an important threat at all.

TABLE C.7

Survey Respondents' Perceived Threats

	C	I	M	NI	NR
a. Nuclear weapon attacks	282	257	299	214	SV: 90 CS Alum: 25 DIB: 21
b. International terrorist attacks	207	332	351	166	SV: 84 CS Alum: 24 DIB: 22
c. Cyberattacks	750	226	78	13	SV: 80 CS Alum: 21 DIB: 20
d. Armed conflicts between nations	192	361	356	148	SV: 87 CS Alum: 23 DIB: 21
e. Armed conflicts within nations	164	307	390	197	SV: 84 CS Alum: 24 DIB: 22
f. Global climate change	730	155	87	91	SV: 80 CS Alum: 24 DIB: 21
g. International financial instability	313	396	280	69	SV: 84 CS Alum: 25 DIB: 21
h. Rising military capabilities in potentially hostile foreign countries	270	350	304	128	SV: 89 CS Alum: 26 DIB: 21

NOTE: The order of these questions was randomized in the survey. Response scale: a critical threat (C); an important but not critical threat (I); a moderate threat (M); or not an important threat at all (NI); no response (NR).

CS Alum = Alumni of Top CS Universities; SV = Silicon Valley.

8. Would you say that the following represent a very serious threat to the United States, a moderately serious threat, just a slight threat, or no threat at all?

TABLE C.8

Survey Respondents' Perceived Threats from Specific Countries

	VS	M	S	NT	NR
a. North Korea	106	285	469	182	SV: 93 CS Alum: 30 DIB: 23
b. Russia	406	424	162	46	SV: 99 CS Alum: 27 DIB: 24
c. China	537	332	131	41	SV: 97 CS Alum: 27 DIB: 23
d. Iran	109	295	414	207	SV: 105 CS Alum: 30 DIB: 28

NOTES: The order of these questions was randomized in the survey. Response scale: very serious threat (VS); moderately serious threat (M); slight threat (S); no threat (NT); no response (NR).

CS Alum = Alumni of Top CS Universities; SV = Silicon Valley.

SECTION G. This section describes a variety of hypothetical world events.

9. Please indicate how justified you think the United States would be in using military force in response to each of the following events.

TABLE C.9

Survey Respondents' Perceived Justification for Military Actions

	J	SJ	N	SU	U	NR
a. A foreign government has attacked American territory and killed American civilians.	875	112	37	11	11	SV: 91 CS Alum: 29 DIB: 21
b. A U.S. Navy ship has been attacked and American sailors have been killed.	684	248	76	23	15	SV: 91 CS Alum: 29 DIB: 21
c. An American adversary has invaded and seized populated territory from a neighboring nation.	246	367	249	126	58	SV: 91 CS Alum: 29 DIB: 21
d. An American adversary has invaded and seized unpopulated territory, such as a small island, from a neighboring nation.	103	241	295	231	175	SV: 92 CS Alum: 29 DIB: 21
e. An American adversary has invaded and forcibly changed the government of a neighboring nation.	247	379	235	120	65	SV: 91 CS Alum: 29 DIB: 21

	J	SJ	N	SU	U	NR
f. To protect an oppressed population from abuses committed by their government.	151	390	282	139	83	SV: 91 CS Alum: 29 DIB: 21
g. To break an economic embargo an American adversary is using to coerce another nation.	83	249	281	233	198	SV: 92 CS Alum: 29 DIB: 21
h. To defend a NATO ally which has requested assistance against foreign aggression.	647	291	79	17	12	SV: 91 CS Alum: 29 DIB: 21
i. To defend a non-NATO ally, such as Saudi Arabia or the Philippines, which has requested assistance against foreign aggression.	192	372	290	119	73	SV: 91 CS Alum: 29 DIB: 21
j. To uphold the requirements of an international treaty.	341	403	210	56	35	SV: 92 CS Alum: 29 DIB: 21
k. To enforce a UN resolution	295	391	223	82	54	SV: 92 CS Alum: 29 DIB: 21
l. To preempt an expected attack by an adversary on American soldiers deployed abroad	232	346	225	135	107	SV: 91 CS Alum: 29 DIB: 21

NOTES: The order of these questions was randomized in the survey. Response scale: justified (J); somewhat justified (SJ); neutral (N); somewhat unjustified (SU); unjustified (U); no response (NR).

CS Alum = Alumni of Top CS Universities; SV = Silicon Valley.

SECTION H. The questions in this section ask about how you interact with mass media, such as news, television, radio, and websites, among other sources. Please read each question carefully and select the most appropriate response for each item.

10. In general, how much trust and confidence do you have in the mass media—such as newspapers, TV, and radio—when it comes to reporting the news fully, accurately, and fairly?

TABLE C.10
Survey Respondents' Trust Levels in Media

A Great Deal	A Fair Amount	Not Very Much	None At All	No Response
80	494	345	128	SV: 90 CS Alum: 29 DIB: 21

NOTE: CS Alum = Alumni of Top CS Universities; SV = Silicon Valley.

11. Please indicate how often you get your news about current events, world affairs, and science and technology developments from the following sources.

TABLE C.11

Survey Respondents' Frequency of Getting News

	Every Day	Several Times per Week	Occasionally	Never	No Response
Websites of news organizations	571	286	156	33	SV: 90 CS Alum: 30 DIB: 21
Podcasts	109	194	386	357	SV: 90 CS Alum: 30 DIB: 21
Blogs	73	157	423	392	SV: 91 CS Alum: 30 DIB: 21
Social media sites	211	216	318	300	SV: 91 CS Alum: 30 DIB: 21
Print newspapers	71	66	283	625	SV: 91 CS Alum: 30 DIB: 21
Television	84	125	322	514	SV: 91 CS Alum: 30 DIB: 21
Radio	74	137	285	549	SV: 91 CS Alum: 30 DIB: 21
Print news magazines	15	66	274	690	SV: 91 CS Alum: 30 DIB: 21
Discussions with your friends and family	118	389	474	64	SV: 91 CS Alum: 30 DIB: 21

NOTE: CS Alum = Alumni of Top CS Universities; SV = Silicon Valley.

SECTION I. Demographic Information

12. What is your age?
- 18–25 years old   133   11.2%
- 26–30 years old   218   18.3%
- 31–35 years old   197   16.6%
- 36–40 years old   169   14.2%
- 41–45 years old   101   8.5%
- 45+ years old   218   18.3%
- No response   152   12.8%

Response Versus No Response
- Silicon Valley Employees   625 / 101

- Alumni of Top CS Universities   222 / 30
- DIB   179 / 21

13. What is your gender?
- Male   883   74.3%
- Female   99   8.3%
- Prefer not to say   63   5.3%
- No response   143   12%

Response Versus No Response
- Silicon Valley Employees   634 / 92
- Alumni of Top CS Universities   223 / 29
- DIB   178 / 22

14. In what state or U.S. territory do you live?
- California   280   23.5%
- Colorado   27   2.3%
- District of Columbia / Maryland / Virginia   59   5.0%
- Florida   21   1.8%
- Massachusetts   46   3.9%
- New Jersey / New York   95   8.0%
- Pennsylvania   32   2.7%
- Texas   54   4.5%
- Washington   277   23.3%
- Other   145   12.2%
- No response   152   12.8%

Response Versus No Response
- Silicon Valley Employees   627 / 99
- Alumni of Top CS Universities   221 / 31
- DIB   178 / 22

15. What is the highest degree or level of school you have completed?
- Did not finish high school   0   0%
- High school diploma or GED   5   0.4%
- Some college or 2-year degree   35   2.9%
- Bachelor's degree   509   42.8%
- Master's degree   346   29.1%
- Doctorate degree   148   12.4%
- No response   145   12.2%

Response Versus No Response
- Silicon Valley Employees   632 / 94
- Alumni of Top CS Universities   223 / 29
- DIB   178 / 22

16. Have you ever served in the armed forces of the United States?
- Yes, currently on active duty   0   0%
- Yes, currently in National Guard or Reserves   2   0.2%
- Yes, retired   8   0.7%
- Yes, separated or discharged   47   3.9%
- Never served in the U.S. armed forces   988   83.0%
- No response   143   12.0%

Response versus No Response
- Silicon Valley Employees   636 / 92
- Alumni of Top CS Universities   223 / 29
- DIB   178 / 22

17. Have you ever served in the armed forces of another country?
- Yes, currently on active duty   0   0%
- Yes, currently in Reserves   9   0.8%
- Yes, retired   6   0.5%
- Yes, separated or discharged   13   1.1%
- Never served in the armed forces of another country   1,017   85.6%
- No response   143   12.0%

Response versus No Response
- Silicon Valley Employees   634 / 92
- Alumni of Top CS Universities   223 / 29
- DIB   178 / 22

18. Which of the following people, if any, served in the military of any country? Please select all that apply.
- My father   307   25.8%
- My mother   21   1.8%
- My sibling   77   6.5%
- My spouse or significant other   23   1.9%
- Other person/people close to me   346   29.1%
- None   483   40.1%
- No response   143   12.0%

Response versus No Response
- Silicon Valley Employees   634 / 92
- Alumni of Top CS Universities   223 / 29
- DIB   178 / 22

19. What is your job type or discipline?
- Software Developer   801   67.3%
- Program Management   43   3.6%
- Test/Quality Assurance (QA)   12   1.0%

- Operations   8   0.7%
- Research   77   6.5%
- Sales   11   0.9%
- Marketing   7   0.6%
- Recruiting   0   0%
- Legal   3   0.3%
- Finance   3   0.3%
- Human Resources (HR)   2   0.2%
- Other   76   6.4%
- No response   145   12.2%

Response Versus No Response
- Silicon Valley Employees   632 / 94
- Alumni of Top CS Universities   223 / 29
- DIB   178 / 22

20. What is your management level?
- Individual Contributor (not managing the careers of other employees)   754   63.5%
- Lead or Manager (managing a group or team of fewer than 35 people)   47   20.8%
- Executive or Senior Leader (managing a group of 35 people or more)   42   3.5%
- No Response   145   12.2%

Response Versus No Response
- Silicon Valley Employees   632 / 94
- Alumni of Top CS Universities   223 / 29
- DIB   178 / 22

21. How many years have you been employed in your current job?
- 0–2 years   338   28.5%
- 3–5 years   306   25.8%
- 6–10 years   217   18.3%
- 10+ years   166   14.0%
- No response   161   13.6%

Response Versus No Response
- Silicon Valley Employees   623 / 103
- Alumni of Top CS Universities   219 / 33
- DIB   175 / 25

22. How many years have you been employed in the technology industry?
- 0–2 years   90   7.6%
- 3–5 years   180   15.1%
- 6–10 years   283   23.8%
- 10+ years   478   40.2%
- No response   157   13.2%

Response versus No Response
- Silicon Valley Employees   624 / 102
- Alumni of Top CS Universities   221 / 31
- DIB   176 / 24

23. Are you employed full time or part time at your current position? If you have more than one position, please think of the one where you work the most hours.
- Full time (35 or more hours per week)   973   81.9%
- Part time (fewer than 35 hours per week)   61   5.1%
- No response   154   13.0%

Response versus No Response
- Silicon Valley Employees   629 / 97
- Alumni of Top CS Universities   220 / 32
- DIB   175 / 25

Abbreviations

AI	artificial intelligence
CIA	Central Intelligence Agency
CEO	chief executive officer
CS	computer science
CSET	Center for Security and Emerging Technology
DIB	Defense Industrial Base
DoD	U.S. Department of Defense
IDC	International Data Corporation
MoE	margin of error
ML	machine learning
NATO	North Atlantic Treaty Organization
NGO	nongovernmental organization
NPR	National Public Radio
NSA	National Security Agency
QA	quality assurance
R&D	research and development
UN	United Nations
VVT&E	verification, validation, test, and evaluation

Bibliography

Acharaya, Ashwin, and Zachary Arnold, *Chinese Public AI R&D Spending: Provisional Findings*, Washington, D.C.: Center for Security and Emerging Technology, December 2019.

Aiken, Catherine, Rebecca Kagan, and Michael Page, "'Cool Projects' or 'Expanding the Efficiency of the Murderous American War Machine?'" Center for Security and Emerging Technology, issue brief, November 2020.

Bass, Dina, and Joshua Brustein, "Big Tech Swallows Most of the Hot AI Startups," *Bloomberg News*, March 16, 2020. As of June 30, 2021:
https://www.bloomberg.com/news/articles/2020-03-16/big-tech-swallows-most-of-the-hot-ai-startups

"Best Global Universities for Computer Science in the United States," *U.S. News and World Report*, 2019.

Blume, Susanna, and Molly Parrish, *Make Good Choices, DoD*, Washington, D.C.: Center for a New American Security, November 20, 2019.

Brenan, Megan, "Cyberterrorism Tops List of 11 Potential Threats to the United States," Gallup, March 22, 2021.

Cameron, Dell, and Kate Conger, "Google Is Helping the Pentagon Build AI for Drones," *Gizmodo*, March 6, 2018.

Cellan-Jones, Rory, "Stephen Hawking—Will AI Kill or Save Mankind?" *BBC News*, October 20, 2016.

Cohen, Jacob, *Statistical Power Analysis for the Behavioral Sciences*, 2nd ed., New York: Academic Press, 1988.

Conger, Kate, "Google Employees Resign in Protest Against Pentagon Contract," *Gizmodo*, May 14, 2018. As of June 30, 2021:
https://gizmodo.com/google-employees-resign-in-protest-against-pentagon-con-1825729300

Conger, Kate, and Cade Metz, "Tech Workers Now Want to Know: What Are We Building This For?" *New York Times*, October 7, 2018. As of June 30, 2021:
https://www.nytimes.com/2018/10/07/technology/tech-workers-ask-censorship-surveillance.html

Colby, Elbridge, and David Ochmanek, "How the United States Could Lose a Great-Power War," *RAND Blog*, October 30, 2019. As of June 30, 2021:
https://www.rand.org/blog/2019/10/how-the-united-states-could-lose-a-great-power-war.html

DoD—*See* U.S. Department of Defense.

Doubleday, Justin, "New Analysis Finds Pentagon Annual Spending on AI Contracts Has Grown to $1.4B," *Inside Defense*, September 24, 2020.

Dougherty, Chris, "Why America Needs a New Way of War," Center for a New American Security, June 12, 2019.

Fan, Weimiao, and Zheng Yan, "Factors Affecting Response Rates of the Web Survey: A Systematic Review," *Computers in Human Behavior*, Vol. 26, No. 2, 2010, pp. 132–139.

Finley, Klint, "Microsoft CEO Defends Army Contract for Augmented Reality," *Wired*, February 25, 2019.

Freedberg, Sydney, Jr., "Google Helps Chinese Military, Why Not US? Bob Work," *Breaking Defense*, June 26, 2018.

Gallup, "Confidence in Institutions," survey database, undated-a, As of June 30, 2021:
https://news.gallup.com/poll/1597/confidence-institutions.aspx

Gallup, "Media Use and Evaluation," webpage, undated-b. As of June 30, 2021:
https://news.gallup.com/poll/1663/media-use-evaluation.aspx

Gramlich, John, "Young Americans Are Less Trusting of Other People—and Key Institutions—Than Their Elders," Pew Research Center, August 6, 2019.

Grinstein, Amir, and Arieh Goldman, "Characterizing the Technology Firm: An Exploratory Study," *Research Policy*, Vol. 35, 2006, pp. 121–143.

Gulati, Ranjay, and Maxim Sytch, "Does Familiarity Breed Trust? Revisiting the Antecedents of Trust," *Managerial and Decision Economics*, Vol. 29, Nos. 2–3, 2008, pp. 165–190.

Hao, Karen, "The Two-Year Fight to Stop Amazon from Selling Face Recognition to the Police," *Technology Review*, June 12, 2020.

International Data Corporation, "IDC Forecasts Improved Growth for Global AI Market in 2021," press release, Needham, Mass., February 23, 2021.

Kantor, Jodi, Karen Weise, and Grace Ashford, "Inside Amazon's Employment Machine," *New York Times*, June 15, 2021.

Lohr, Steve, "At Tech's Leading Edge, Worry About a Concentration of Power," *New York Times*, September 26, 2019.

Macrotrends, "Alphabet: Number of Employees 2006–2021/GOOG," webpage, undated-a. As of February 10, 2022:
https://www.macrotrends.net/stocks/charts/GOOG/alphabet/number-of-employees

Macrotrends, "Microsoft: Number of Employees 2006–2021/MSFT," webpage, undated-b. As of February 10, 2022:
https://www.macrotrends.net/stocks/charts/MSFT/microsoft/number-of-employees

Mattis, James, *Summary of the 2018 National Defense Strategy of the United States of America*, Washington, D.C.: U.S. Department of Defense, 2018.

"Mercenaries vs. Missionaries: John Doerr Sees Two Kinds of Internet Entrepreneurs," *Knowledge@Wharton*, blog post, April 13, 2000. As of February 10, 2022:
https://knowledge.wharton.upenn.edu/article/mercenaries-vs-missionaries-john-doerr-sees-two-kinds-of-internet-entrepreneurs

Metz, Cade, "Tech Giants Are Paying Huge Salaries for Scarce AI Talent," *New York Times*, October 22, 2017.

National Security Commission on Artificial Intelligence, *Final Report of the National Security Commission on Artificial Intelligence*, Arlington, Va., March 2021.

Office of the Director of National Intelligence, *Annual Threat Assessment of the U.S. Intelligence Community*, Washington, D.C., April 9, 2021.

Pew Research Center, "Public Trust in Government: 1958–2021," survey database, May 17, 2021. As of June 30, 2021:
https://www.pewresearch.org/politics/2021/05/17/public-trust-in-government-1958-2021/

Piper, Kelsey, "The Case for Taking AI Seriously as a Threat to Humanity," *Vox*, October 15, 2020.

Poulson, Jack, "Reports of a Silicon Valley/Military Divide Have Been Greatly Exaggerated," *Tech Inquiry*, July 7, 2020.

Rainie, Lee, Scott Keeter, and Andrew Perrin, *Trust and Distrust in America*, Washington, D.C.: Pew Research Center, July 22, 2019. As of February 10, 2022:
https://www.pewresearch.org/politics/2019/07/22/trust-and-distrust-in-america/

Sargent, John, and Marcy Gallo, *The Global Research and Development Landscape and Implications for the Department of Defense*, Washington, D.C.: Congressional Research Service, R45403, June 28, 2021.

Schafer, Amy, *Generations of War*, Washington, D.C.: Center for a New American Security, May 8, 2017.

SeekOut, "Searching with SeekOut: People Insights," webpage, undated. As of February 10, 2022:
https://support.seekout.io/hc/en-us/articles/360053596452-Using-People-Insights-to-Source-More-Strategically

Shane, Scott, and Daisuke Wakabayashi, "'The Business of War': Google Employees Protest Work for the Pentagon," *New York Times*, April 4, 2018.

Shlapak, David A., and Michael Johnson, *Reinforcing Deterrence on NATO's Eastern Flank: Wargaming the Defense of the Baltics*, Santa Monica, Calif.: RAND Corporation, RR-1253-A, 2016. As of June 30, 2021:
https://www.rand.org/pubs/research_reports/RR1253.html

Smeltz, Dina, Ivo Daalder, Karl Friedhoff, Craig Kafura, and Brendan Helm, *Rejecting Retreat: Results of the 2019 Chicago Council Survey of American Public Opinion and U.S. Foreign Policy*, Chicago: Chicago Council on Global Affairs, September 16, 2019.

Spohr, Dominic, "Fake News and Ideological Polarization: Filter Bubbles and Selective Exposure on Social Media," *Business Information Review*, Vol. 34, No. 3, 2017, pp. 150–160.

SSRS, opinions about Donald Trump, telephone survey conducted for CNN, January 20, 2020. As of February 10, 2022:
https://cdn.cnn.com/cnn/2020/images/01/20/rel1a.-.trump,.impeachment.pdf

Statt, Nick, "Google Walkout Organizer Claire Stapleton Tells Her Story of the Company's Retaliation," *Wired*, December 12, 2019. As of June 30, 2021:
https://www.theverge.com/2019/12/19/21030681/google-claire-stapleton-walkout-organizer-retaliation-essay-go-read-this

Sull, Donald, Charles Sull, and Andrew Chamberlain, *Measuring Culture in Leading Companies*, Cambridge, Mass.: MIT Sloan Management Review, 2019.

Tarraf, Danielle C., William Shelton, Edward Parker, Brien Alkire, Diana Gehlhaus, Justin Grana, Alexis Levedahl, Jasmin Leveille, Jared Mondschein, James Ryseff, Ali Wyne, Daniel Elinoff, Edward Geist, Benjamin N. Harris, Eric Hui, Cedric Kenney, Sydne Newberry, Chandler Sachs, Peter Schirmer, Danielle Schlang, Victoria M. Smith, Abbie Tingstad, Padmaja Vedula, and Kristin Warren, *The Department of Defense Posture for Artificial Intelligence: Assessment and Recommendations*, Santa Monica, Calif.: RAND Corporation, RR-4229-OSD, 2019. As of June 29, 2021:
https://www.rand.org/pubs/research_reports/RR4229.html

Tung, Liam, "Google: Here's Why We're Pulling Out of Pentagon's $10bn JEDI Cloud Race," ZDNet, October 9, 2018.

U.S. Department of Defense, "DOD Adopts Ethical Principles for Artificial Intelligence," press release, February 24, 2020. As of June 26, 2021:
https://www.defense.gov/Newsroom/Releases/Release/Article/2091996/
dod-adopts-ethical-principles-for-artificial-intelligence

White House, *Interim National Security Strategic Guidance*, Washington, D.C., March 2021. As of September 3, 2021:
https://www.whitehouse.gov/wp-content/uploads/2021/03/NSC-1v2.pdf

Zhang, Baobao, and Allan Dafoe, "U.S. Public Opinion on the Governance of Artificial Intelligence," *Proceedings of the AAAI/ACM Conference on AI, Ethics, and Society*, New York, February 7–8, 2020, pp. 187–193.

Zhang, Baobao, Markus Anderljung, Lauren Kahn, Noemi Dreksler, Michael Horowitz, and Allan Dafoe, "Ethics and Governance of Artificial Intelligence: Evidence from a Survey of Machine Learning Researchers," *Journal of Artificial Intelligence Research*, Vol. 71, 2021.